JavaScript

20 Lessons to Successful Web Development

About the Author

Robin Nixon is a prolific author on programming and web development (as well as psychology and motivation), with his books having been translated into numerous foreign languages—frequently topping the US and international computer book charts. He has worked with computers and technology for all his life, and began writing about the subject about 35 years ago.

He has authored hundreds of articles and over two dozen books, and is a popular video and online instructor, with thousands of students taking his courses. Robin is also an accomplished programmer, developer, and entrepreneur, with several successful Internet startups to his name, from which he has learned a wealth of programming hints and tips, which he enjoys passing on in his expanding range of web development books, including the following titles:

- *CSS & CSS3: 20 Lessons to Successful Web Development* (McGraw-Hill Education, 2015)
- *HTML5: 20 Lessons to Successful Web Development* (McGraw-Hill Education, 2015)
- *PHP: 20 Lessons to Successful Web Development* (McGraw-Hill Education, 2015)
- *Learning PHP, MySQL, JavaScript, CSS & HTML5* (O'Reilly, 2014)
- *Web Developer's Cookbook* (McGraw-Hill Education, 2012)
- *HTML5 for iOS and Android* (McGraw-Hill Education, 2010)

About the Technical Editor

Albert Wiersch has been writing software since the Commodore VIC-20 and Commodore 64 days in the early 1980s. He holds a Bachelor of Science degree in Computer Science Engineering and an MBA from the University of Texas at Arlington. Albert currently develops and sells software that helps web developers, educators, students, businesses, and government agencies check their HTML and CSS documents and their websites for quality problems, including many SEO (search engine optimization), mobility, and accessibility issues, with discounts made available to students. His website is at *HTMLValidator.com*.

JavaScript

20 Lessons to Successful Web Development

Robin Nixon

New York   Chicago   San Francisco
Athens   London   Madrid   Mexico City
Milan   New Delhi   Singapore   Sydney   Toronto

Cataloging-in-Publication Data is on file with the Library of Congress

McGraw-Hill Education books are available at special quantity discounts to use as premiums and sales promotions, or for use in corporate training programs. To contact a representative, please visit the Contact Us pages at www.mhprofessional.com.

JavaScript: 20 Lessons to Successful Web Development

1234567890   DOC DOC   10987654

ISBN   978-0-07-184158-0
MHID   0-07-184158-X

Sponsoring Editor
Brandi Shailer

Editorial Supervisor
Patty Mon

Project Manager
Anupriya Tyagi,
Cenveo® Publisher Services

Acquisitions Coordinator
Amanda Russell

Technical Editor
Albert J. Wiersch

Copy Editor
Manish Tiwari,
Cenveo Publisher Services

Proofreader
Lisa McCoy

Indexer
Ted Laux

Production Supervisor
Jean Bodeaux

Composition
Cenveo Publisher Services

Illustration
Cenveo Publisher Services

Art Director, Cover
Jeff Weeks

Cover Designer
Jeff Weeks

To Julie

Contents at a Glance

Contents

x Contents

Acknowledgments

Once again I would like to thank the amazing team at McGraw-Hill Education, with whom it is always a real pleasure to work on new book projects. In particular, I would like to thank my Sponsoring Editor Brandi Shailer, Amanda Russell for overseeing the project's development, Editorial Supervisor Patty Mon, Production Supervisor Jean Bodeaux, Copy Editor Manish Tiwari, and Jeff Weeks for the excellent cover design. Thanks also goes again to Albert Wiersch (whom I have had the pleasure of working with on a number of occasions) for his meticulous eye for detail during technical review.

Introduction

Why This Book?

The concept for this book grew out of Robin's extremely popular online courses in which thousands of students are enrolled. From their feedback, it became evident that the reason for this popularity was that students love the way the material is broken up into easy-to-digest lessons, each of which can be completed in an hour or less. They also like the no-nonsense, jargon-free, and friendly writing style.

Now, working together, Robin and McGraw-Hill Education have revised, updated, and developed his JavaScript course into this book, which not only will teach you everything you need to learn in 20 lessons (of less than an hour each), but it also includes an average 15-minute detailed video walk-through for each lesson, comprising 5 hours of footage in total.

Watch the videos after reading the lesson to reinforce key concepts, or use the video as a primer to working through each print lesson. Together, the book and videos make learning JavaScript easier than it has ever been, and is the ideal way for you to add JavaScript skills to your web development toolkit.

 To view the accompanying video for this lesson, please visit mhprofessional.com/nixonjavascript/.

Who Should Read This Book

Each chapter is laid out in a straightforward and logical manner as a lesson, with plenty of examples written using simple and clear JavaScript. Before moving on to each subsequent lesson, you have the opportunity to test your new knowledge with a set of 10 questions about what you have just learned. You can also work along with every lesson by watching its accompanying video tutorial.

Even if you have never programmed before, you will still learn everything you need from this book, because the principles behind how programming works are fully explained, and no prior knowledge is ever assumed. Between the lessons, the self-test questions, and the videos, this book will ensure that you learn the language thoroughly and quickly.

To save you typing them in, all the example files from the book are saved in a freely downloadable zip file available at the companion website: *20lessons.com*.

What This Book Covers

This book covers every aspect of JavaScript, starting with basic syntax and language rules, such as where and how you can include JavaScript in your web documents. You will also learn about numeric and string variables, arrays, and objects, and how to assign, manipulate, and read values. More advanced techniques such as using hashes to index into objects and multidimensional arrays are also made easy. How to loop code and control program flow with conditional statements is explained in plain English, as well as how to create and use functions and methods in either a procedural or object-oriented manner. Important techniques such as handling mouse and keyboard events, managing cookies and local storage, and running background tasks and Ajax communication are all revealed in simple, short examples. By the time you finish the book's 20 lessons, you'll have a thorough grounding in JavaScript and be able to use it to dynamically enhance your web pages.

How to Use This Book

This book has been written in a logical order so that each lesson builds on information learned in the previous ones. You should begin at Lesson 1 and then work sequentially through the book, proceeding to the next lesson only when you can correctly answer the self-test questions in the previous one.

Lessons should take you less than an hour to finish, including viewing the accompanying video walk-through provided with each one. With over 5 hours of video in total, that's an average of 15 minutes dedicated to each lesson.

How Is This Book Organized?

This book takes you right from the basics through to advanced techniques and includes the following lessons: Introduction to JavaScript, Incorporating JavaScript into a Web Page, Working with Arithmetic Operators and Functions, Applying Comparison and Logical Operators, Creating JavaScript Arrays, Accessing Multidimensional Arrays, Calling Array Functions, Pushing to and Popping from Arrays, Advanced Array Manipulation, Controlling Program Flow, Looping Sections of Code, Writing Functions, Manipulating JavaScript Objects, Handling Errors and Regular Expressions, Interacting with the Document Object Model, Inserting Inline JavaScript and Events, Controlling Cookies and Local Storage, Working with Different Browsers, Implementing Interrupts and Timeouts, and Using Ajax. Appendix A contains the answers to self-test questions, and Appendix B covers a handy reference to the most commonly used JavaScript functions and properties.

PART I

JavaScript Basics

1

Introduction to JavaScript

 To view the accompanying video for this lesson, please visit mhprofessional.com/nixonjavascript/.

At the dawn of the Internet, webmasters were a strange breed (and few and far between) and nobody really knew what their mastery entailed. But their development toolkit was nothing compared to what we have today; they had a knowledge of HTML (HyperText Markup Language) and a basic understanding of the HTTP (HyperText Transfer Protocol) interface for serving up web pages, and really that was all—there actually wasn't a lot to building web pages.

You see, there were no such things as plug-ins or style sheets, and the Web was actually quite a dull and drab experience as a consequence, but it was so new and fascinating that design, layout, and dynamic interactivity weren't important. All users wanted was more and more information (and funny cat pictures). In fact, what most casual web users probably know today would likely have been considered webmaster skills in the early 1990s.

But time marches on and, in the case of the Web, it does so at Internet Time (which is several times faster than normal), and pretty soon the latest browsers supported loading plug-ins for greater functionality, such as playing audio or video, style sheets were adopted to vastly improve the display of fonts and web layout and design, new graphical enhancements were developed such as the animated GIF (graphics interchange format), and probably most important of all was the introduction of a scripting language.

It was realized quite early on that, as powerful as HTML was, it simply didn't offer the interactivity that users were calling out for. Something new was needed, but what? Clearly a programming language of some sort had to be the answer, but not just any old language—a new one would have to be designed from the ground up in order to hook directly into HTML, so that the two could work together seamlessly. And that language came to be known as *JavaScript*.

In the Beginning

The JavaScript programming language was written by Brendan Eich at Netscape and was previously known by both of the names Mocha and LiveScript. It was first incorporated into the Netscape Navigator browser (see Figure 1-1) in 1995, at the same time that Netscape added support for Sun's Java technology.

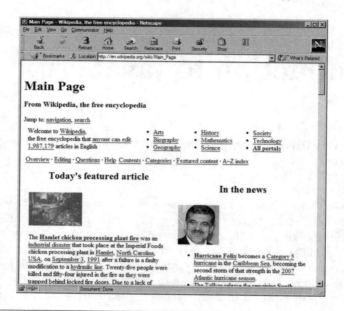

FIGURE 1-1   Netscape Navigator 4.08

JavaScript is a quite different language from Java, but, as part of a marketing deal made between Netscape and Sun Microsystems, it was given its name to try and benefit from the general buzz surrounding the Java language.

To justify this naming, in JavaScript, all Java keywords are reserved, its standard library follows Java's naming conventions, and its Math and Date objects are based on Java 1.0 classes. Also, the trademark name JavaScript belongs to Oracle, but the similarities end there.

Note   Because the name JavaScript is trademarked (by Oracle since its purchase of Sun, which developed Java), when the language was submitted to ECMA, the European Computer Manufacturers Association (a nonprofit standards organization), the standard was *officially* given the name ECMAScript. However, you rarely hear people referring to the standard as such in general use (*ECMAScript* simply doesn't have the same ring to it as *JavaScript*). Technically, therefore, both JavaScript and JScript are dialects of ECMAScript, but in the same way that the trademarked word Aspirin fell into common use for acetylsalicylic acid in many countries, all dialects of this scripting language tend to be referred to simply as JavaScript.

Microsoft's version, called *JScript*, was released a year later as a component of Internet Explorer (IE) 3.0 and, as you might expect, it differed in several important respects, making it less than 100 percent compatible with JavaScript. Unfortunately, that remains true to this day; although IE9 addressed many of the prior incompatibilities and IE10 became even more compatible with the other browsers, IE11 (the latest at the time of writing, see Figure 1-2) still retains a number of niggling differences that developers have to take into account.

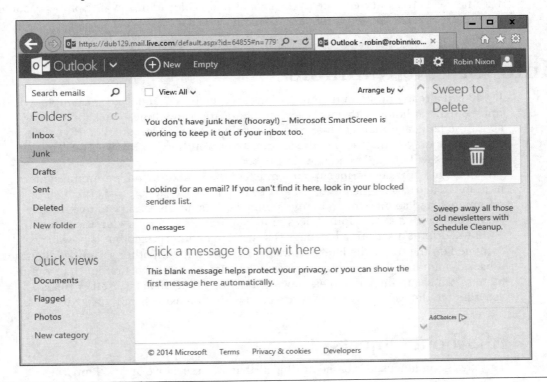

FIGURE 1-2   Microsoft Internet Explorer 11

In-browser Scripting

Unlike other languages used for creating websites, such as Perl, PHP, and Ruby, JavaScript runs within the web browser and not on a web server. This makes it the perfect tool for creating dynamic web pages because it can modify HTML elements in real time. It is also the technology behind Web 2.0 Ajax functionality, in which data is transferred between a web server and web browser behind the scenes, without the user being aware of it.

JavaScript's great power lies in its ability to access HTML's Document Object Model (DOM), in which every element on a web page can be individually addressed (either reading or modifying its value), and elements can also be created and deleted on the fly, as well as layered over each other and moved about.

You can even go so far as to treat a web browser window as a blank canvas and build entire applications and arcade games from scratch, using JavaScript and the DOM (although it takes some quite advanced programming skills). What's more, with new HTML5 features such as the canvas and geolocation, JavaScript has become even more of a backbone for modern, dynamic web pages.

Info for Programmers

If you can already program in another language such as C or Java, for example, you'll find yourself at home with JavaScript, and here are a few things you should know about the language that will make your learning process even quicker. If you are not a programmer, you may skip to the section "Why You Need to Know JavaScript," as these terms will be explained later in the book.

To begin with, JavaScript supports much of the structured programming syntax used in C, such as `if()` statements, `while()` and `for()` loops, `switch()` statements, and so on. Unlike many languages, it is not necessary to terminate statements with a semicolon, unless more statements will follow on the same line.

JavaScript is a scripting language that used to be interpreted but is nowadays compiled on the fly by the latest browsers. In common with other scripting languages, it uses dynamic typing in which types are associated with values rather than variable names. Values are interpreted as integers, floating point, strings, or other types according to the way in which they are used within an expression.

All About Objects

The JavaScript language is based on objects that are associative arrays. Properties of objects can be accessed using either the period operator (for example, `object.height`) or with square brackets (for example, `object['height']`). Object properties can be enumerated using `for(... in ...)` loops.

In JavaScript, functions are themselves objects, so they have properties such as `length` and methods such as `call()`. This means they may also be assigned to variables, passed as arguments, and returned by other functions. Functions are referenced by naming them without parentheses (for example, `a = funcname`) or invoked by adding the parentheses (for example, `a = funcname()`).

The former case sets the variable `a` to contain a copy of the function object with the name `funcname`, whereas the latter assigns the result returned by calling the function to the variable `a`. You may create inner functions within other functions, and these retain the scope of the outer function, including its constants, local variables, and argument values.

Rather than implementing classes, JavaScript uses prototypes for inheritance. Functions can double as object constructors, and prefixing a function with the new keyword creates a new object, calling that function with its local this keyword.

Why You Need to Know JavaScript

Although it is possible to get by with a basic knowledge of HTML and maybe a smattering of CSS (Cascading Style Sheets), if you are at all serious about developing professional-looking websites that attract repeat visitors and build an audience, then there's no getting around the fact that you have to learn JavaScript in order to access all the latest goodies your users will expect.

Following is a list of just some of the features you may wish to include in a web page, and which require the use of JavaScript to one extent or another:

- **Animations**   Some animation can be achieved with CSS transitions, but for true interactivity, you need to control graphics directly using JavaScript.
- **Geolocation**   To provide location-aware services to your users, you must access the data using JavaScript.
- **Canvas**   The only way to draw on the HTML5 canvas is with JavaScript commands.
- **Audio and Video**   You can add these with simple HTML5 tags, but to control playback directly, you will need JavaScript.
- **Form Processing**   If you wish to make your forms easier to use by having in-browser validation, user prompting, and error checking, then you have to do much of this with JavaScript, although HTML5 is making some great inroads in this direction.
- **Ajax**   Any behind-the-scenes communication with a web server you need to make has to be done via JavaScript calls.
- **Dynamic Elements**   Some elements can be changed via CSS and mouse-overs, but for anything more, such as resizing, moving, or dragging and dropping, you have to use JavaScript.
- **In-browser Gaming**   Games that run in the browser without plug-ins such as Flash are written in JavaScript (see Figure 1-3).
- **Floating Elements**   Pop-ups and other floating elements that follow the page as you scroll are all implemented with JavaScript.
- **Hover Effects**   Thumbnail or advanced tooltips that hover over HTML elements are created and controlled with JavaScript.

And this list is by no means exhaustive; just take a look at *tinyurl.com/ cooljsexamples* to see some very clever features that have been built with JavaScript, or check out everyday websites such as Facebook, Gmail, and Twitter, all of which subtly use JavaScript behind the scenes to provide their slick interfaces.

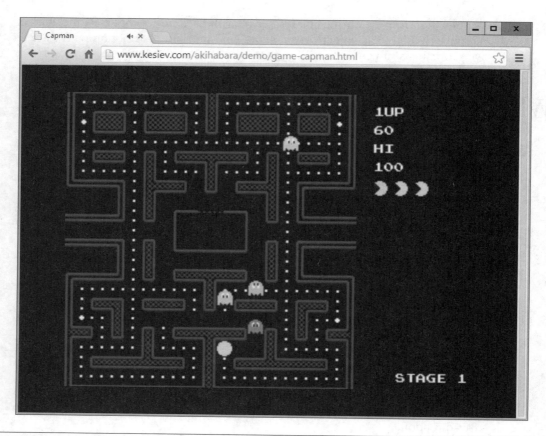

FIGURE 1-3   A Pacman-style game written in JavaScript

For example, if you have a Gmail account, next time you log in, right-click and select the View Source option in your browser to see how the page is constructed. As well as all the JavaScript files that Gmail calls up from its server, the main web page itself is completely packed with JavaScript, as shown in Figure 1-4.

But don't let that picture put you off, Google packs its JavaScript as tightly as possible to save on bandwidth and to make it difficult for the casual observer to determine what's going on. I guarantee that the original source code will be neatly laid out one line at a time and clearly documented so that a team of programmers can work with it. It's probably only when the time comes to publish an update that the nice and tidy code gets run through another program to squish it into production web pages.

FIGURE 1-4   Viewing Gmail's JavaScript source code

Summary

As I said, if you are new to programming, don't worry about any of these terms because I explain them later in the book at the appropriate places. And I promise, they are just words, and their use will become second nature to you as you learn JavaScript, because it really is a simple language to learn.

Self-Test Questions

Test how much you have learned in this lesson with these questions. If you don't know an answer, go back and reread the relevant section until your knowledge is complete. You can find the answers in Appendix A.

1. What is the name of the official language of which JavaScript and Jscript are dialects?

2. From where does JavaScript get its name?

3. Who owns the trademark for the JavaScript name?

4. Why did a new programming language have to be invented?

5. What does the acronym HTML stand for?

6. What does the acronym HTTP stand for?

7. What does the acronym CSS stand for?

8. What does the acronym DOM stand for?

9. On what are JavaScript's Math and Date objects based?

10. How can you view the source HTML/JavaScript of a web page?

Incorporating JavaScript into a Web Page

 To view the accompanying video for this lesson, please visit mhprofessional.com/ nixonjavascript/.

The whole point of JavaScript is that it is designed to offer dynamic functionality to what previously were static web pages. Therefore, JavaScript code is generally embedded within the web page to which it applies. This can be in the form of embedding the code directly in the HTML document itself, or by means of a tag that tells the browser the location of a file containing some JavaScript to load in and execute. This external file may be on the same or a different web server.

Additionally, the location within a web page at which you insert the JavaScript (or link to a JavaScript file) becomes the default location in which any output from the JavaScript will be inserted. Of course, because it is a programming language, you can tell it exactly where in a web page to display anything, but if you use a simple JavaScript function such as `write()`, it will insert whatever is written in the current location.

Therefore, for this and other reasons, where you place your JavaScript can be important, and I will explain how you can choose the right location a little later on. First, though, let's take a look at the basics.

Using Comments

Before looking at the JavaScript language and its syntax, I want to introduce the commenting feature. Using comments, you can add text to a JavaScript program that explains what it does. This will help you later when you are debugging, and is especially helpful when other people have to maintain code that you write.

There are two ways to create a comment in JavaScript, the first of which is to preface it with two slashes, as follows:

```
// This is a comment
```

You can place a comment after a JavaScript statement, like this:

```
anumber = 42 // Assigns 42 to anumber
```

Or, if you wish to temporarily restrict a line of code from executing, you can insert a comment tag before it and the statement will be completely ignored, like this:

```
// anumber = 42
```

Sometimes you need to be able to comment out more than a single line of text. In this case, you can use the multiline form of commenting in which you start the comment with /* and end it with */, like this:

```
/* This is a multi-line
   set of comments, which
   can appear over any
   number of lines      */
```

 As well as supporting extensive documentation, this form of commenting lets you temporarily comment out complete blocks of code by simply placing the start and end tags as required—something that can be extremely helpful when debugging.

Using Semicolons

If you like, you may add a semicolon after every JavaScript statement, and many programmers choose to do this. However, I prefer not to because semicolons are not mandatory. On the other hand, if you wish to place more than one statement on a single line, you must separate them with a semicolon. Therefore, for example, the three following sets of code are all valid syntax:

```
a = 1
b = 2

a = 1; b = 2

a = 1;
b = 2;
```

However, the following is not valid, as JavaScript will not know how to make sense of it due to the omission of a semicolon:

```
a = 1 b = 2
```

Think of the semicolon as acting like a newline as far as the JavaScript interpreter is concerned (or vice versa). If in doubt, always add one and, although you may end up with more semicolons than you need, at least your code will run correctly (assuming no other errors). In this book, however, I use semicolons only where they are necessary.

Where to Place the JavaScript Code

As previously mentioned, where you place your JavaScript code can make a difference. For example, if you wish default output to go straight into the current document, you may choose to place your JavaScript directly within the `<body>` and `</body>` tags. On the other hand, if you have a very long web page that takes more than a second or so to load, you might choose to place your JavaScript code within the `<head>` and `</head>` tags, so that it will be executed as soon as that part of the document is loaded in.

In the Document Head

To insert your JavaScript within the head of a document, you must place `<script>` and `</script>` tags where the script is to go, like this (highlighted in bold text):

```html
<html>
  <head>
    <title>Page Title</title>
    <script>
      // Your JavaScript goes here
    </script>
  </head>
  <body>
    The document body goes here
  </body>
</html>
```

In the Document Body

To insert your JavaScript within the body of a document, you must place `<script>` and `</script>` tags where the script is to go, like this (highlighted in bold text):

```html
<html>
  <head>
    <title>Page Title</title>
  </head>
  <body>
    The document body goes here
```

```
  <script>
    // Your JavaScript goes here
  </script>
</body>
</html>
```

Including JavaScript Files

If you wish to keep your JavaScript code separate from your document contents (something you are likely to want to do once your JavaScript starts to become any length other than small), you can place it in its own file (usually with the file extension *.js*) and, instead of inserting script between <script> and </script> tags, you would include the code like this (highlighted in bold text):

```
<html>
  <head>
    <title>Page Title</title>
    <script src='myscript.js'></script>
  </head>
  <body>
    The document body goes here
  </body>
</html>
```

If the script file is not in the current directory, you must include the path along with the filename, like this:

```
<script src='pathtofolder/myscript.js'></script>
```

Or if the code is on another server, include the correct http:// (or https:// prefix, domain, and path) like this:

```
<script src='http://server.com/folder/script.js'></script>
```

When including a script rather than embedding it in a web document, you may still choose where you wish to insert it, for example, into the body rather than the head, like this:

```
<html>
  <head>
    <title>Page Title</title>
  </head>
  <body>
    <script src='myscript.js'></script>
    The document body goes here
  </body>
</html>
```

When you include an external JavaScript file this way, you must not have any `<script>` or `</script>` tags in the included document because a `<script>` tag has already been used to pull the file in.

JavaScript Language Syntax

I've already discussed some of the *syntax* used by the JavaScript language, such as how to comment out sections of code and where semicolons need to be used. But what is meant by syntax? Well, it's a set of rules that define how to correctly structure a JavaScript program.

In this section I'll outline the major syntax issues so that when you start programming, you'll introduce the minimum of errors, so please forgive me if there's a little overlap with earlier sections.

Case Sensitivity

JavaScript is what is known as a case-sensitive language. This means that it distinguishes between the use of the uppercase (`A-Z`) and lowercase letters (`a-z`). Therefore, for example, the variable `MyVariable` is quite different from `myvariable` (variables being special names used to stand in for values such as numbers or strings of characters, explained a little further on).

JavaScript will treat these as two totally different variables, so you need to be careful when choosing your variable names. Generally, I observe the following guidelines so that I can more easily go back and understand code I may have written in the past:

- All global variables that are accessible anywhere in a program are set to all uppercase, such as `HIGHSCORE`.
- Temporary variables used in loops are single letters in lowercase, such as `j`.
- Function names use a capital letter at the start of each word, like this: `MyFunctionName()`.

This is only a naming convention that I use, and you may choose to apply different uppercase and lowercase rules to this, or simply stick to all lowercase—it's entirely up to you.

Whitespace

Any spaces and tabs are known as *whitespace*, and any combination of these is usually treated by JavaScript as if it were a single space. The exception is when they are placed inside quotation marks, in which case they form part of a string, and all the characters are used.

Newline or carriage return characters are also treated as whitespace by JavaScript (unless within quotes), except that each one creates an implied semicolon, which, as you saw in the previous section, is used to denote the end of a statement. Therefore, for example, the statement a = b + c is valid on a single line, but if you format it as follows, a will be assigned the value in b and then an implied semicolon will be added, so that the + c line following is then interpreted on its own, causing a syntax error:

```
a = b
+ c
```

Variables

A variable in any programming language is simply a container for a value. For example, imagine that you have a few empty plastic pots into which you can place items (see Figure 2-1). Think of these as a metaphor for variables, in that you can take a small piece of paper and write the number 42, for example, on it and insert it into one of the pots. If you then take a marker pen and write MyVariable on the pot, it is just like a JavaScript variable being set using this line of code:

```
MyVariable = 42
```

FIGURE 2-1   An empty pot and blank piece of paper

Figure 2-2 shows the pot now labeled and the paper written on. You can now manipulate this variable in a variety of ways. For example, you can add another value to it, like this:

```
MyVariable = MyVariable + 13
```

FIGURE 2-2   The pot has been labeled and the paper written on.

This has the effect of adding 13 to the value of 42 already stored in the variable so that the result is 55, the new value held in the variable. This is analogous to taking the piece of paper with the number 42 written on it out of the pot labeled MyVariable, noting the value, adding 13 to it, and then replacing that piece of paper with another one on which you have written the number 55 (see Figure 2-3), which you then place back into the pot.

55

FIGURE 2-3   A new slip of paper with the number 55 on it

Likewise, you might issue the following command, for example, that will multiply the current value in the variable (55) by the value 3: MyVariable = MyVariable * 3. Again, this is equivalent to taking the paper from the pot, performing the multiplication, and placing a new piece of paper with the result of 165 (see Figure 2-4) back into the pot.

165

FIGURE 2-4   Another piece of paper with the number 165 on it

All the time the current numeric value is updated and popped inside the pot with the label MyVariable on it, so that any time that value needs to be referenced (looked up), the pot can simply be opened and the slip of paper inside then read.

Variable Naming

There are a number of rules governing how you use the JavaScript programming language. For instance, variables must begin with either an uppercase or lowercase letter (A-Z or a-z), or the $ or _ symbols. No other character may begin a variable name (except for some Unicode characters, but these should generally never be used in variable names).

Variables may not contain any mathematical operators (such as + or *), punctuation (such as ! or &), or spaces, but after the first character, they may include the digits 0-9 or any of the characters that can begin a variable name. All JavaScript keywords (such as window, open, string, and so on) are reserved and may not be used as variable names (although they can be used as *part* of a variable name, such as mywindow or string3).

String Variables

When a variable is used to store a number (as in the preceding examples), it's known as a *numeric variable*. However, it's also possible to store text in a variable, in which case the variable is called a *string variable* (because sequences of characters are called strings in programming languages).

Examples of strings include the name "Bill Smith", the sequence of characters "A23bQ%j", and even the characters "123" that, in this case, are a string of digits, not the number 123 (because of the quotes).

In the same way that you can store a number in a variable, so you can a string, and you use the same method of assignment, like this:

```
Name = "Mary Jones"
```

Notice the use of double quotation marks around this string. These are what tell JavaScript that the value is a string and is how you can assign the string "123" to a variable, as opposed to the number 123, for example. In terms of the pot and paper metaphor, the preceding statement is equivalent to labeling a new pot as "Name" and writing "Mary Jones" on a piece of paper that you place in it, as shown in Figure 2-5.

FIGURE 2-5   This pot is labeled "Name" and contains a string value.

Obviously, you can't perform arithmetic on strings, but there are other actions you can take, such as shortening them; adding more characters to the front, middle, or end; extracting a portion of a string value; and more. For example, you can concatenate two strings together (attach one to the other) using the same + operator you use for performing additions, like this:

```
Singer = "Pharrell"
Singer = Singer + " Williams"
```

The result of these two statements is to concatenate the string "Pharrell" (first assigned to and then read from the variable Singer) with the string " Williams" and place the resulting string back into the variable Singer. Lesson 4 shows some other operations you can perform on strings.

Using Quotation Marks in Strings

You have seen the use of the double quote character to indicate the start and end of a string, but you may also use the single quote if you prefer, like this:

```
Dinner = 'Fish and Chips'
```

The end result is identical, whichever type of quotation marks you use.

But there is a good reason why you may choose one type instead of the other, and that's when you need to include a particular quotation mark within a string. For example, suppose you needed to store the string "Isn't the weather fine?". As it stands, using double quotation marks works just fine, but what would happen if you surrounded the string with single quotation marks instead, like this: 'Isn't the weather fine?'?

Well, you would get a syntax error because JavaScript would see only the string 'Isn' and then some gibberish following it, like this: t the weather fine?'.

Then again what about the string `'Jane said, "Hello"'`? This time, this string works using single quotes, but because of the double quotes within it, if you were to surround the string with double quotes like this, `"Jane said, "Hello""`, JavaScript would see one string, like this: `"Jane said, "`, some gibberish (to JavaScript) like this: `Hello`, and another string with nothing in it, like this: `""`. It would give up at all this and generate an error.

 Placing a pair of quotes together with nothing between them results in what is called the *empty string*. It is commonly used for erasing or initializing the value of a string variable.

Escaping Characters

But things can get more interesting, because what about the occasions when you might require both types of quotes to be included within a string, like this: `"Mark said, "I can't wait""`? As it stands, this string will cause a syntax error, but you can easily fix it using the escape character, which is simply a backslash, like this: `"Mark said, \"I can't wait\""`.

What the escape character does is tell JavaScript to ignore the `\` character and to use the character following it as a string element, and not a string container.

You may escape either of the quotation marks inside a string to ensure they are used only as string elements, and can also use escape characters to insert other characters that you cannot easily type in such as tabs and newlines, as follows:

- `\'` – single quote
- `\"` – double quote
- `\\` – backslash
- `\b` – backspace
- `\f` – form feed
- `\n` – newline
- `\r` – carriage return
- `\t` – tab

Variable Typing and Casting

In JavaScript, unlike some other programming languages, a variable can change its type automatically. For example, a string can become a number, and vice versa, according to the way in which the variable is referenced. For example, take the following assignment in which the variable `MyVar` is given the string value of `"12345"`:

```
MyVar = "12345"
```

Although the string is created from a group of all digits, it is a string. However, JavaScript is smart enough to understand that sometimes a string can be a number, so in the following assignment it converts the string value in `MyVar` to a number prior to applying the subtraction, and then the resulting value (which is now the number 12000) is stored back in MyVar, which is now a numeric variable:

```
MyVar = MyVar - 345
```

Likewise, a number can be automatically converted to a string, as in the following two lines, which first set the numeric variable Time to the value 6, then the string " O'clock" is appended to the number value in Time, which is first turned into a string to make this string concatenation possible:

```
Time = 6
Time = Time + " O'clock"
```

The result is that Time is now a string variable with the value "6 O'clock".

Because of this changing of variables from one type to another (known as automatic type casting), it is not actually correct to think of JavaScript variables in terms of type, so I will no longer do so. Instead, you should consider only their contents and how JavaScript will interpret them.

However, sometimes it is necessary for you to force the type of a variable. For example, consider the following statement and ask yourself what you think JavaScript will do with it:

```
MyVar = "12345" + 678
```

If you think it will turn the string "12345" into a number and then add 678 to it (to result in the number 13023), you are unfortunately wrong. Although that might seem the appropriate action, JavaScript chooses to turn the number 678 into the string "678" and then concatenate it with "12345", resulting in the string "12345678". If this is the result you want, then that's good, but if not, then you must force the type that JavaScript should use by using the function Number(), like this:

```
MyVar = Number("12345") + 678
```

Now, before you say, "Why not simply make the string a number in the first place?" consider the case of already having the variable MyVar, whose contents may be either a string or number (and you do not know which), but you then must add a number to it (rather than append a string) like this:

```
MyVar = MyVar + 678
```

If MyVar happens to be a string, a concatenation will occur, but if it is a number, an addition will take place. In this case, it is necessary to use the Number() function to ensure you always get the correct result intended, like this:

```
MyVar = Number(MyVar) + 678
```

Note   If you know for sure that you are only using numbers in a particular variable and it will never contain anything else, you will not need to use the Number() function to cast the value. Generally, the occasions on which you will find it beneficial to use casting are when dealing with values over which you have less control, such as user input that you are processing.

The Cast Functions

The following three functions are available for forcing the type of a variable (or casting it):

- **Boolean()**   Cast the value to either `true` or `false`.
- **Number()**   Cast the value to a number.
- **String()**   Cast the value to a string.

Values that are cast to Boolean can become one of only two values: `true` or `false`. Any string of at least one character in length, any object, or any number other than 0 will be cast to the value `true`. An empty string, the number 0, and the values `undefined` or `null` result in the value `false`.

When a value is cast to a number, if it is a string containing characters other than digits (or for another reason it cannot be converted to a number), then the JavaScript value NaN (for Not a Number) will be returned by `Number()`, instead of a number. Because NaN values cannot have arithmetic operations performed on them, any attempt to do so will see the value remain as NaN, so the following results in `MyVar` containing the value NaN, and not the value 23, as you might expect:

```
MyVar = Number("A string") + 23
```

The `String()` function is the most flexible in that it can safely turn any value into a string, even including JavaScript values such as `NaN`, `null`, `undefined`, `true`, and `false`.

Summary

We've actually covered quite a lot of ground in this lesson, which has explained some of the simpler JavaScript syntax and data handling capabilities. In the following lesson, we'll start to see how these come together with operators to enable you to start creating simple JavaScript expressions.

Self-Test Questions

Test how much you have learned in this lesson with these questions. If you don't know an answer, go back and reread the relevant section until your knowledge is complete. You can find the answers in Appendix A.

1. How do you create a single-line comment and a multiline comment?

2. Do you need to end lines of code with semicolons?

3. Name three places you can put JavaScript code in a web document.

4. Is JavaScript case-sensitive or case-insensitive?

5. Which characters can you use in a variable name?

6. With which operator do you add two values together?

7. With which operator do you concatenate two objects into a string?

8. How can you incorporate the same quotation mark within a string that encloses it?

9. How can you change a string to a number?

10. What does NaN stand for?

:

Working with Arithmetic Operators and Functions

To view the accompanying video for this lesson, please visit mhprofessional.com/ nixonjavascript/.

In the previous lesson, you saw a few examples of operators in action, such as the + sign used either for addition or for concatenating strings together, the – sign used for subtraction, and the = operator used for assigning values.

But JavaScript supports many more operators than that, such as `*`, `/`, and more, and also includes functions you can use for more advanced expression evaluation, such as `Math.sin()`, `Math.sqrt()`, and many others. In this lesson I'll explain all of these, how they work, and how to use them.

This is an important lesson as it covers much of the foundation of how JavaScript works, so even if you have programmed before using another language, I recommend you read this thoroughly, because there are a number of things JavaScript handles in a unique manner.

Arithmetic Operators

The arithmetic operators in JavaScript are the ones that allow you to create numeric expressions, and there are more than simply addition, subtraction, multiplication, and division, as shown in Table 3-1.

You can try these operators out for yourself by loading the file *math_operators.htm* from the companion archive into a browser, which should look like Figure 3-1. Try changing the various values and operators applied, and check the results you get.

The first four of these operators should be very clear to you, so I'll only explain the last three, starting with the modulus operator, `%`. What this operator returns is simply

TABLE 3-1 The Arithmetic Operators

Operator	Description	Example	Result
+	Addition	3 + 11	14
–	Subtraction	9 – 4	5
*	Multiplication	3 * 4	12
/	Division	21 / 7	3
%	Modulus (*remainder after division*)	21 % 8	5
++	Increment	a = 5; ++a	(a *equals*) 6
– –	Decrement	a = 5; – –a	(a *equals*) 4

the remainder after calculating a division. For example, the modulus of 12 and 4 (calculated using the expression 12 % 4) is 0, because 4 goes into 12 an exact number of times, and therefore there is no remainder.

On the other hand, the modulus of 24 and 5 (calculated as 24 % 5) is 4, because 5 goes into 24 four times (5 multiplied by 4 is 20), leaving a remainder of 4, the modulus of the expression.

Now let's look at the increment and decrement operators. These come in tremendously handy because without them you would have to write expressions like this:

```
a = a + 1
```

This is cumbersome when you only want to increment (or decrement) a value by 1, and so the creators of JavaScript allow you to use the following syntax instead:

```
++a
```

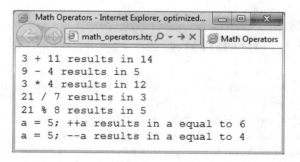

FIGURE 3-1   The arithmetic operators in use

I'm sure you will agree this is much shorter and sweeter. It also comes with fringe benefits because the increment and decrement operators can be used within flow control commands such as `if()` statements (which I explain in full detail in Lesson 10, but will give you a sample here).

Consider the following code, which assumes that `Time` contains a 24-hour time value between 0 and 23, and which is set up to trigger once an hour, on the hour (using code not shown here, but which is assumed to be in place):

```
Time = Time + 1
document.write('The time is ' + Time)
if (Time < 12) document.write('AM')
else            document.write('PM')
```

This code first increments the value in `Time` by 1, because this code has been called on the hour, so it's now one hour since the last time it was called, and so `Time` must be updated. Then on the next line it displays the time in the browser (using a call to the `document.write()` function) prefaced by The time is .

After that, an `if()` statement is reached, which tests the variable `Time` to see whether it currently has a value of less than 12. If so, then it must still be the morning and so the string `AM` is output. Otherwise, it's the afternoon and so `PM` is displayed— fairly straight-forward stuff.

 This is a simple version of the `if()` statement in that it has only a single statement after the `if`, and there is also only a single one after `else`. Therefore, no curly braces are used to enclose the action statements. Please see Lesson 10 for greater detail on using `if()` and `else` with multistatement actions.

However, programmers always like to write the tightest and cleanest code possible, and so the following code is considered better programming practice, as it removes an entire line of code, like this (with the incremented variable and operator highlighted):

```
document.write('The time is ' + ++Time)

if (Time < 12) document.write('AM')
else            document.write('PM')
```

Pre-incrementing

What has occurred in the previous example is an instance of *pre-incrementing* the variable `Time`. In other words, before the value in `Time` is used, it is incremented. Only after this incrementing is the current value in `Time` used for displaying in the `document.write()` statement.

In Figure 3-2 these three lines of code have been called three times, with an original starting value for `Time` of 9 (using the file *inc_and_dec.htm* from the companion archive).

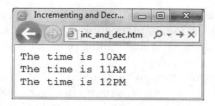

FIGURE 3-2   Using the increment operator

Post-incrementing

You may also place the ++ increment operator after a variable name, and then it is known as *post-incrementing*. What happens when you do this is that the value in the variable being incremented is looked up before the increment, and that value is used by the code accessing it. Only after this value has been looked up is the variable incremented.

The following code illustrates this type of incrementing by displaying both the before and after values in the variable a (with instances of the variable and increment operator highlighted):

```
document.write('a was ' + a++ + ' and is now ' + a)
```

Working through this statement from left to right, first the string a was is output, then a++ is displayed. This results in the current value of a being displayed, and only then is a incremented. After this the string and is now is output, followed by the new value in a, which now contains the incremented value from the earlier increment operation. Therefore, if a had an initial value of 10, the following is displayed:

```
a was 10 and is now 11
```

Pre- and Post-decrementing

You can use the decrement operator in exactly the same way as the increment operator, and it can either be placed before a variable for pre-decrementing or after for post-decrementing. Following are two examples that both display the same but achieve the result using pre-decrementing for the first and post-decrementing for the second (with instances of the variable and decrement operator highlighted):

```
document.write('b was ' + b + ' and is now ' + --b)
document.write('b was ' + b-- + ' and is now ' + b)
```

Here, if b had an initial value of 10, the following is displayed:

```
b was 10 and is now 9
b was 9 and is now 8
```

Note If it's still not entirely clear which type of increment or decrement operator to use out of pre- and post-methods, don't worry; just use the pre-methods (with the operator before the variable) for now, because it will become obvious to you when the time comes that you actually have a need to use the post-method (with the operator after the variable).

Arithmetic Functions

To accompany the arithmetic operators, JavaScript comes with a library of arithmetic functions you can call on, as follows (the initial uppercase M in `Math` is necessary because JavaScript is case-sensitive):

- `Math.abs(a)`   Returns a as a positive number (or 0 if a is 0).
- `Math.acos(a)`   Returns the arccosine of a.
- `Math.asin(a)`   Returns the arcsine of a.
- `Math.atan(a)`   Returns the arctangent of a.
- `Math.atan2(a,b)`   Returns the arctangent of a / b.
- `Math.ceil(a)`   Rounds up to return the integer closest to a.
- `Math.cos(a)`   Returns the cosine of a.
- `Math.exp(a)`   Returns the exponent of a (`Math.E` to the power a).
- `Math.floor(a)`   Rounds down to return the integer closest to a.
- `Math.log(a)`   Returns the log of a base e.
- `Math.max(a,b)`   Returns the maximum of a and b.
- `Math.min(a,b)`   Returns the minimum of a and b.
- `Math.pow(a,b)`   Returns a to the power b.
- `Math.random()`   Returns a floating point random number greater than or equal to 0, but less than 1 (from 0 to 0.999...).
- `Math.round(a)`   Rounds up or down to return the integer closest to a.
- `Math.sin(a)`   Returns the sine of a.
- `Math.sqrt(a)`   Returns the square root of a.
- `Math.tan(a)`   Returns the tangent of a.

You should be familiar with most of these. For example, to return the square root of 64, you use the following:

```
Math.sqrt(64) // Returns 8
```

But there are a couple that need a little more explaining, such as `Math.abs()`. What this does is take any value (negative, zero, or positive), and if it is negative, turn it into a positive value, like this:

```
Math.abs(27) // Returns 27
Math.abs(0)  // Returns 0
Math.abs(-5) // Returns 5
```

The other function needing extra explanation is `Math.random()`. This returns a floating point value with a statistically random value (although not truly random) between 0 and 1. Therefore, for example, if you have to emulate a 12-sided dice, you must multiply the result of the function call and turn it into an integer, like this:

```
Math.floor(Math.random() * 12) // Returns 0 - 11
```

This expression returns a value between 0 and 11.999 recurring, which is first turned into an integer, by dropping the floating point part of the number using the `Math.floor()` function. The result is a value between 0 and 11.

 If, for example, you need your random number to be a value between 1 and 12 (rather than 0 through 11), simply add 1 to this result.

Assignment Operators

Like many other languages, JavaScript likes to help you out by offering more efficient ways to achieve results. One of these ways is by letting you combine assignment and arithmetic operators into six different types of assignment operators.

This typically saves lines of code and makes your program code much easier to write, and for others to understand.

Table 3-2 lists the assignment operators available, provides examples of them in use, and shows the result of doing so when the variable a already contains the value 21. You can see the result of using the expressions in this table in Figure 3-3, created with the example file *assignment_operators.htm* from the accompanying archive.

TABLE 3-2 The Assignment Operators

Operator	Description	Example	Result
=	Simple assignment	a = 21	21
+=	... with addition	a = 21; a += 5	26
-=	... with subtraction	a = 21; a -= 2	19
*=	... with multiplication	a = 21; a *= 3	63
/=	... with division	a = 21; a /= 10	2.1
%=	... with modulus	a = 21; a %= 4	1

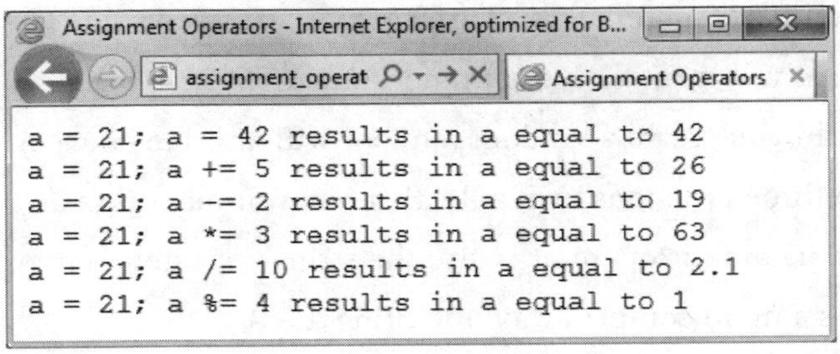

```
Assignment Operators - Internet Explorer, optimized for B...   ⊟  ▣  ✕
←  →  🔗 assignment_operat  🔍 ▼ → ✕   🔗 Assignment Operators  ✕
a = 21; a = 42 results in a equal to 42
a = 21; a += 5 results in a equal to 26
a = 21; a -= 2 results in a equal to 19
a = 21; a *= 3 results in a equal to 63
a = 21; a /= 10 results in a equal to 2.1
a = 21; a %= 4 results in a equal to 1
```

FIGURE 3-3   Using the various assignment operators

Therefore, for example, instead of using a = a + 5, you can use the more compact a += 5. And you can use assignment operators in conjunction with other expressions and variables, as with the following example, which results in a having a value of 15 (10 + (25 / 5)):

```
a   = 10
b   = 25
a += (b / 5)
```

Summary

By now you should be seeing how JavaScript is actually quite a simple and graceful language, with many similarities to the natural flow of English (and similar written languages). Using it should be making good sense to you, especially now that you can make a wide range of mathematical operations—the core of any computer language.

In the following chapter we will turn our attention to comparison and logical operators, which you can use to make decisions, the second most important ability a computer language provides.

Self-Test Questions

Test how much you have learned in this lesson with these questions. If you don't know an answer, go back and reread the relevant section until your knowledge is complete. You can find the answers in Appendix A.

1. What does the ++ operator do?

2. What is the difference between ++a and a++?

3. What is the purpose of the % operator?

4. Which operator assigns a value to a variable?

5. What operator increments a variable by a specified value?

6. How can you turn a value from negative to positive?

7. How can you create a random number with a value between 1 and 60 inclusive?

8. Which three functions turn a floating point number into an integer?

9. Which arithmetic operator is also the string concatenation operator?

10. What is a more compact way of writing a = a / 20?

4

Applying Comparison and Logical Operators

 To view the accompanying video for this lesson, please visit mhprofessional.com/nixonjavascript/.

The arithmetic and string operators you have so far seen are fundamental to manipulating data inside computers. But without the ability to test things and make decisions, computers would be little more than advanced calculators. However, when you bring comparison and logical operators into the equation, you begin to expand the JavaScript language into a form with which complex tasks can be broken down, analyzed, and implemented.

Combining these with the arithmetic and string operators, you then have most of the basic features of a programming language, and from this point you simply extend the language by adding the ability to control program flow (as explained in Lesson 10), including data structures such as arrays (see Lesson 5), supporting sequences of instructions in functions (see Lesson 12), or offering even greater abstractions such as creating objects containing both data and program code (as explained in Lesson 13).

Therefore, once you have finished this lesson, you will already be programming at a basic level.

Comparison Operators

One of the most important processes that happens in a program is comparison. For example, possibly the most frequent type of construct used goes along the lines of *if this then do that*. The job of comparison operators is to figure out the *this* part, and there are eight of them, as listed in Table 4-1.

TABLE 4-1   The Comparison Operators

Operator	Description	Example	Result
==	Equal to	1 == 1	true
===	Equal in value and type	1 === '1'	false
!=	Not equal to	1 != 2	true
!==	Not equal in value and type	1 !== '1'	true
>	Greater than	1 > 2	false
<	Less than	1 < 2	true
>=	Greater than or equal to	1 >= 1	true
<=	Less than or equal to	2 <= 1	false

Figure 4-1 shows several different comparison operators used on different values and the results obtained. It was created using the file *comparison_operators.htm*, available in the companion archive.

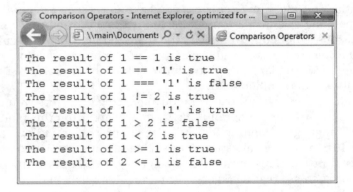

FIGURE 4-1   A selection of comparison operators in use

If you haven't programmed before, some of these operators may seem a little confusing, especially seeing as we are taught as children that = is the equal to operator. However, in programming languages such as JavaScript, the = is used as an assignment operator, and therefore code would become harder to read (and the writers of programming languages would have a much harder time figuring out its meaning) if the = symbol were also used to make comparisons. Therefore, the == operator is used for comparisons instead, like this:

```
if (a == 12) // Do something
```

In JavaScript, however, the types of variables are loosely defined and it's quite normal, for example, to ask whether the number 1 is the same as the string '1', because the string '1' can be used either as a string or as a number depending on the context. Therefore, the following expression will return the value true:

```
if (1 == '1') // Results in the value true
```

 JavaScript uses the internal values of true and false to represent the result of making comparisons such as the preceding, and you can use the keywords true and false in your programming to check for these values.

Progressing through the list of comparison operators, when you wish to determine whether two values are the same value and *also* of the same type, you can use the === operator, like this:

```
if (1 === '1') // Results in the value false
```

Similarly, you can test whether values are *not* equal (but not comparing the type) using the != operator, like this:

```
if (1 != 2)    // Results in the value true
if (1 != '1') // Results in the value false
```

And if you wish to check whether two values are not equal in *both* value and type, you use the !== operator, like this:

```
if (1 !== '1') // Results in the value true
```

The remaining comparison operators test whether one value is greater than, less than, greater than or equal to, or less than or equal to another, like this:

```
if (1 > 2)  // Results in the value false
if (1 < 2)  // Results in the value true
if (1 >= 1) // Results in the value true
if (2 <= 1) // Results in the value false
```

Logical Operators

JavaScript supports three logical operators with which you can extend your *if this* parts of code even further, as listed in Table 4-2.

TABLE 4-2   The Logical Operators

Operator	Description	Example	Result
&&	And	1 == 1 && 2 == 2	true
||	Or	1 == 1 || 2 == 3	true
!	Not	!(1 == 1)	false

Figure 4-2, created using the file *logical_operators.htm* from the companion archive, shows these operators being used in expressions.

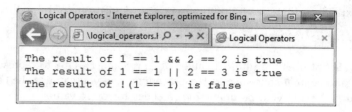

FIGURE 4-2   Using logical operators

The `&&` operator (known as the *and* operator) allows you to test for multiple conditions being `true`, saving you from having to write multiple lines of code by combining them into a single expression, like this:

```
if (a == 4 && b == 7) // Do this
```

In this example, the statement following the `if ()` (just a comment in this instance) will be executed only if a has a value of 4 and also b has a value of 7. Or you can test whether at least one value is `true` using the `||` operator (known as the *or* operator), like this:

```
if (a == 4 || b == 7) // Do this
```

Here if either a has the value 4 or b has the value 7, the statement after the `if ()` will be executed, so only one of the expressions needs to evaluate to `true`. Finally, you can negate any expression using the `!` symbol (known as the *not* operator) by placing it in front of the expression (generally placing the expression within parentheses too, so that the `!` applies to the entire expression instead of only to a part of it), like this:

```
if (!(game == over)) // Carry on playing
```

In this example, if the variable game contains the same value as the variable over, the result of the expression is `true`. Then the `!` operator negates this to turn that value into `false`. Therefore, the statement after the `if ()` will not be executed.

On the other hand, if game is not equal to over, the expression evaluates to `false`, which is negated to `true`, and so the code after the `if ()` is executed. Therefore, the expression equates to the semi-English sentence "If not game over then do this."

Note When an expression can only return either a `true` or `false` value, it is known as a *Boolean expression*. When combined with *and*, *or*, and *not* (`&&` and `||` and `!`), such expressions are said to use Boolean logic.

The Ternary Operator

Ever on the lookout for ways to make program code simpler and more compact, program language developers also came up with a thing called the *ternary operator*, which allows you to combine "If this then do that thing otherwise do another thing" type logic into a single expression, like this:

```
document.write(game == over ? 'Game over' : 'Keep playing')
```

The way the ternary operator works is that you provide an expression that can return either `true` or `false` (a Boolean expression). Following this, you use a ? character, after which you place the two options, separated with a : character, as follows:

```
expression ? do this : do that
```

For example, another ternary expression might go like the following, which sets the string variable AmPm to either AM or PM, according to the numeric value in the variable Time:

```
AmPm = Time < 12 ? 'AM' : 'PM'
```

Bitwise Operators

There is a type of operator supported by JavaScript that as a beginner to programming you are most unlikely to use, due to it being quite advanced, and that's the bitwise operator. This type of operator acts on the individual 0 and 1 bits that make up binary numbers, and can be quite tricky to use.

The bitwise operators are &, |, ^, ~, <<, >>, and >>>. In order, they support bitwise and, or, exclusive or, not, left-shift, sign-propagating right-shift, and zero-fill right-shift on binary numbers.

The bitwise operators can be combined with the = assignment operator to make a whole new collection of bitwise assignment operators.

However, this is a basic book on JavaScript and not an advanced tutorial, so I won't go into how you use them, because you already have enough new stuff to learn as it is. But for the curious who would like to know more about them, you can check out the following web pages, which cover them in some detail:

- *tinyurl.com/bitwiseops*
- *tinyurl.com/bitwiseops2*

Operator Precedence

In JavaScript some operators are given a higher precedence than others. For example, multiplication has a higher precedence than addition, so in the following expression the multiplication will occur *before* the addition, even though the addition appears first:

```
3 + 4 * 5
```

The result of this expression is 23 (4 × 5 is 20, 3 + 20 is 23). But if there were no operator precedence (with the expression executed simply from left to right), it would evaluate to 35 (3 + 4 is 7, 7 × 5 is 35).

By providing precedence to operators, it obviates the need for parentheses, because the only way to make the preceding expression come out to 23 without operator precedence would be to insert parentheses as follows:

```
3 + (4 * 5)
```

With this concept in mind, the creators of JavaScript have divided all the operators up into varying levels of precedence according to how "important" they are (in that multiplication is considered more "important" than addition due to its greater ability to create larger numbers). For the same reason, division is given greater precedence than subtraction, and so on.

Therefore, unless you intend to use parentheses in all your expressions to ensure the correct precedence (which would make your code much harder to write and for others to understand, due to multiple levels of parentheses), you need to know these precedencies, which are listed in Table 4-3.

TABLE 4-3   Operator Precedence

Precedence	Operators	Precedence	Operators
1	. [] new	10	&
2	()	11	^
3	++ --	12	|
4	! ~ unary+ unary- typeof void delete	13	&&
5	* / %	14	||
6	+ -	15	? :
7	<< >> >>>	16	= += -= *= /= %= <<= >>= >>>= &= ^= !=
8	< <= > >= in instanceof	17	,
9	== != === !==		

There are quite a few operators in this table that you have not yet seen. Some of which (such as the bitwise operators) will not be covered, and others (such as in, typeof, and so on) will be explained later in the book.

All you need to learn from this table, though, is which operators have higher precedence than others, where 1 is the highest and 17 is the lowest precedence, and where an operator has lower precedence but you need to elevate it, all you need to do is apply parentheses in the right places for the operators within them to have raised precedence.

The unary+ and unary- entries in Table 4-3 represent the use of placing either a + before an expression to force it into being used as a number or placing a - sign in front of an expression to negate it (change a negative value to positive or vice versa). The comma operator (at a precedence of 17) is used as an expression or argument separator, so it naturally has the lowest precedence.

Operator Associativity

JavaScript operators also have an attribute known as *associativity*, which is the direction in which they should be evaluated. For example, the assignment operators all have right-to-left associativity because you are assigning the value on the right to the variable on the left, like this:

```
MyVar = 0
```

Because of this right-to-left associativity, you can string assignments together, setting more than one variable at a time to a given value, like this:

```
MyVar = ThatVar = OtherVar = 0
```

This works because associativity of assignments starts at the right and continues in a leftward direction. In this instance, OtherVar is first assigned the value 0. Then ThatVar is assigned the value in OtherVar, and finally MyVar is assigned the value in ThatVar.

On the other hand, some operators have left-to-right associativity, such as the || (or) operator. Because of left-to-right associativity, the process of executing JavaScript can be speeded up, as demonstrated in the following example:

```
if (ThisVar == 1 || ThatVar == 1) // Do this
```

When JavaScript encounters the || operator, it knows to check the left-hand side first. Therefore, if ThisVar has a value of 1, there is no need to look up the value of ThatVar, because as long as one or the other expressions on either side of the || operator evaluates to true, then the entire || expression evaluates to true, so if the left half has evaluated to true, then so has the entire || expression. In cases such as this, the JavaScript interpreter will eagerly skip the second half of the expression, knowing it is running in an optimized fashion. By the way, in programming language theory, this is called *lazy evaluation*.

Knowing whether operators have right-to-left or left-to-right associativity can really help your programming. For example, if you are using a left-to-right associative operator such as ||, you can line up all your expressions left to right from the most to the least important.

Therefore, it is worth taking a moment to familiarize yourself with the contents of Table 4-4 so that you will know which operators have what associativity.

TABLE 4-4   Operator Associativity

Associativity	Operators
Right-to-left	`! ~ unary+ unary- typeof void delete ?: = += -= *= /= %= <<= >>= >>>= &= |=`
Left-to-right	`. [] * / % + - << >> >>> < <= > >= in instanceof == != === !== & ^	&& || ,`

The `with` Keyword

Using JavaScript's `with` keyword, you can simplify some types of JavaScript statements by reducing many references to an object to a single reference. For example, in the following code, the `document.write()` function never references the variable `string` by name:

```
string = "The quick brown fox jumps over the lazy dog"

with (string)
{
   document.write("The string's length is " + length)
   document.write("<br>Upper case: " + toUpperCase())
}
```

Even though `string` is never directly referenced by `document.write()`, this code still manages to output the following:

The string's length is 43 characters
Upper case: THE QUICK BROWN FOX JUMPS OVER THE LAZY DOG

The way this works is that the JavaScript interpreter recognizes that the `length` property and the `toUpperCase()` method have to be applied to some object, but because they stand alone, the interpreter assumes they must apply to the `string` object specified in the `with` statement.

 The very fact that assumptions about which object to apply the `with` to have to be made by the interpreter can make its use ambiguous in some applications. Therefore, I would generally recommend that you try to avoid working with this statement unless you feel confident that you can use it without ambiguity.

Summary

This lesson has brought you up to speed with all you need to know about using operators, so now you're ready to start looking at some of JavaScript's more complex and interesting objects in the following lesson on arrays.

Self-Test Questions

Test how much you have learned in this lesson with these questions. If you don't know an answer, go back and reread the relevant section until your knowledge is complete. You can find the answers in Appendix A.

1. Which operator is used to check whether two values are equal?

2. What is the difference between the == and the === operators?

3. What values can a comparison expression evaluate to?

4. Which operator would you use to test whether two values (or expressions) are both true?

5. Which operator would you use to test whether at least one of two values (or expressions) is true?

6. With which operator can you test whether a value (or expression) is not true?

7. Which operator out of * and + has the highest precedence and will be evaluated first?

8. Which operator has the lowest precedence of all?

9. In which direction do the mathematical operators *, /, +, and − evaluate from?

10. How can you shorten code by removing repeated uses of an object's name?

Creating JavaScript Arrays

 To view the accompanying video for this lesson, please visit mhprofessional.com/
nixonjavascript/.

JavaScript is capable of managing data in a more powerful manner than simply via
variables. One example of this is JavaScript arrays, which you can think of as
collections of variables grouped together. For example, a good metaphor for an array
might be a filing cabinet with each drawer representing a different variable, as shown
in Figure 5-1.

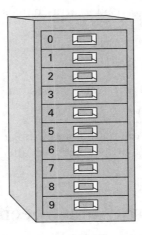

FIGURE 5-1   A filing cabinet representing a 10-element array

41

As with the small pot metaphor in Lesson 2, using a filing cabinet to assign a value, you should imagine writing it down on pieces of paper, placing it in the relevant drawer, and closing it. To read back a value, you open the drawer, take out the paper, read its value, return the paper, and close the drawer. The only difference between the cabinet and the pots is that the drawers of the filing cabinet (representing an array) are all in sequential order, whereas a collection of pots (representing variables) are stored in no particular order.

Although JavaScript arrays can be any size (up to the maximum allowed by the JavaScript engine), for the sake of simplicity I have only shown 10 elements in the figure. You can access each of the elements in an array numerically, starting with element 0 (the top drawer of the cabinet). This index number is important, because you might think that logically the number 1 would be the best starting point, but that isn't how JavaScript arrays are accessed—you should always remember that the first element is the zeroth.

Array Names

The rules for naming arrays are exactly the same as those for naming variables. Array names must begin with either an upper- (A-Z) or lowercase letter (a-z), or the $ or _ symbol. No other character may begin an array name (except for some Unicode characters, but these should generally never be used in variable names).

Array names may not contain any mathematical operators (such as + or *), punctuation (such as ! or &), or spaces, but after the first character, they may include the digits 0-9 or any of the characters that can begin an array or variable name.

All JavaScript keywords (such as `window`, `open`, `string`, and so on) are reserved and may not be used as array names.

Creating an Array

To create an array, you can declare it in advance, like this:

```
MyArray = new Array()
```

This has the effect of creating a new object of the type `Array()` and then calling it `MyArray`. This array object contains no data, but is ready for data to be assigned to its elements.

Creating an Array of a Specific Length

To create an array of a specific length, you provide a single argument to the `Array()` function call, like this:

```
MyArray = new Array(5)
```

This has the effect of creating a new object of the type `Array()`, which contains no data, but has five elements ready to be populated with values.

Assigning Values to an Array Element

You can populate arrays with data (in a similar manner to assigning values to variables) like this:

```
MyArray[0] = 23
MyArray[1] = 67.35
```

Here the integer 23 is assigned to element 0 (the top drawer of the cabinet), whereas the floating point number 67.35 is assigned to the element at index 1 (the second drawer down because indexes begin at 0). In fact, you can assign any legal value to an array element, including strings, objects, and even other arrays (which I come to in Lesson 6), like this:

```
MyArray[3] = "Hello world"
MyArray[4] = new Date()
```

 I explain the use of objects in Lesson 13, but for now, all you need to know is that `MyArray[4]` now contains a `Date` object holding the current date and time.

You are not restricted to assigning values in order, so you can go right in and assign values to any elements, like this:

```
MyArray[9] = "Good morning"
MyArray[7] = 3.1415927
```

In this instance, if the length of `MyArray[]` was previously less than nine elements, its length will automatically be increased to nine by the former of these two assignments.

Using Indexes

The element number used for storing a particular value is known as the array *index*, and you can use integer values (as shown so far) or variable values as indexes. For example, the following first creates a variable and assigns it a numeric value, which is then used to assign another value to the array:

```
MyIndex         = 123
MyArray[MyIndex] = "Good evening"
```

This has the effect of assigning the string value `"Good evening"` to the element with an index of 123 in `MyArray[]`.

Retrieving Values

Once an array has been created and it has been populated with data, to retrieve a value from an array, you simply refer to it, like this:

```
document.write(MyArray[0])
```

This will fetch the value stored in the zeroth element of `MyArray[]` (or the top drawer of the filing cabinet metaphor) and then pass it to the `document.write()` function to display it in the browser. Likewise, you can return a value using a variable, like this:

```
MyIndex = 713
document.write(MyArray[MyIndex])
```

Whatever value is stored in element 713 of the array will then be displayed in the browser.

 The preceding two examples (and many following ones) assume you have already created an array. If you have not previously created an array but try to read from one, an error will be generated and your code will fail.

There are other ways you can use array values, such as assigning them to other variables or other array elements, or using them in expressions. For example, the following code assigns the value 23 to an array element, which is then looked up and used in an expression, in which 50 is added to it and the result (73) is displayed in the browser:

```
MyArray[7] = 23
document.write(MyArray[7] + 50)
```

Or, you may wish to display a value in an alert window using code such as the following, which results in your browser looking like Figure 5-2 (although the style of the window varies by browser):

```
MyArray[7] = 23
alert(MyArray[7] + 50)
```

FIGURE 5-2   Displaying a value in an alert window

Using Array Elements as Indexes

You can even go a step further and use the value stored in an array element as an index into another (or the same) array, like this:

```
OtherArray[0]           = 77
MyArray[OtherArray[0]] = "I love the movie Inception"
```

Here the zeroth element of `OtherArray[]` is assigned the integer value of 77. Once assigned, this element is used as the index into `MyArray[]` (rather like the movie *Inception*, with arrays within arrays). However, this is quite complex programming, and you are unlikely to use these types of indexes as a beginner to JavaScript.

 The fact that you can use any valid integer value (including values in variables, array elements, and those returned by functions) means that you can use mathematical equations to iterate through arrays. For example, as you will discover in Lesson 11, it is easy to create code that runs in a loop to process each element of an array in turn.

Other Ways of Creating Arrays

You have already seen the following type of declaration for creating a JavaScript array:

```
MyArray = new Array()
```

But there are also a couple of other methods you can use, which also have the effect of simplifying your code by allowing you to populate the array with some data at the same time. The first method is as follows:

```
MyArray = new Array(123, "Hello there", 3.21)
```

Here the array `MyArray[]` is created and its first three elements immediately populated with three different values: an integer, a string, and a floating point number. This is equivalent to the following (much longer) code:

```
MyArray      = new Array()
MyArray[0] = 123
MyArray[1] = "Hello there"
MyArray[2] = 3.21
```

You can also go a step further and simplify things right down to their bare bones by using code that implies the creating of an array, without using the new keyword or the `Array()` function, like this:

```
MyArray = [123, "Hello there", 3.21]
```

 Once you have created an array, if you need to apply any more values to elements within it, you must use the standard form of assigning values. If you reuse the short form of combined array creation and value assignment, it will simply reset the array to the values in the assignment.

Using Associative Arrays

Using numeric indexes is all well and good when you only have a few elements in an array to cope with. But once an array starts to hold meaningful amounts of data, using numbers to access its elements can be highly confusing. Thankfully, JavaScript provides a great solution to this by supporting the use of names to associate with array elements, in much the same way that variables have names.

Let's use JavaScript's associative arrays to store the ages of the players in a mixed, under eleven, five-a-side soccer team. Here the array is initialized and then the age of each player is assigned to an element in the array using the players' names:

```
SoccerTeam = new Array()
SoccerTeam['Andy']   = 10
SoccerTeam['Brian']  = 8
SoccerTeam['Cathy']  = 9
SoccerTeam['David']  = 10
SoccerTeam['Ellen']  = 9
```

Having been assigned, these values they can now easily be looked up by name, like this, which displays Cathy's age in the browser:

```
document.write(SoccerTeam['Cathy'])
```

Keys, Values, and Hash Tables

When you use associative arrays, you are actually creating a collection of *key* and *value* pairs. The name you assign to an array element is known as the key, whereas the value you provide to the element is the value.

In other languages (such as PHP), this type of data structure is implemented using a *hash table*. When an object (such as a string) is used as a key for a value, this is called a *hash value* and the data structure is a *hash table*. In Lesson 13, you will learn how all variables in JavaScript are, in fact, objects and that you can access them in a variety of ways, as well as those that have been shown so far (variables, arrays, and associative arrays).

Other Ways of Creating an Associative Array

If you wish, you can use a short from of creating and populating an associative array, like this:

```
SoccerTeam = new Array(
{
   'Andy'  : 10,
   'Brian' : 8,
   'Cathy' : 9,
   'David' : 10,
   'Ellen' : 9
})
```

The syntax here is different from populating a standard array, in that you must enclose the element value assignments in curly braces. If you use the square brackets instead, the statement will fail. Also, rather than using = you use the : operator to assign values.

In fact, you can shorten the syntax even further by having your code *imply* the new keyword and `Array()` function, like this:

```
SoccerTeam =
{
   'Andy'  : 10,
   'Brian' : 8,
   'Cathy' : 9,
   'David' : 10,
   'Ellen' : 9
}
```

I'm sure you'll agree this is much simpler and easier to use, once you know that this type of code structure causes the creation of an array. But you may prefer to stick with the longer form until you are completely happy with using arrays. Also, I have chosen to be liberal with newlines here for reasons of clarity, but if you wish, you can run all these five substatements into a single line.

As with standard variables and arrays, you are not restricted to only storing numbers in associative arrays, because you can assign any valid value, including integers, floating point numbers, strings, and even other arrays and objects. The following illustrates a couple of these:

```
MyInfo =
{
   'Name'       : 'Bill Gates',
   'Age'        : 58,
   'Occupation' : 'Philanthropist',
   'Children'   : 3,
   'Worth'      : 77000000000
}
```

In the preceding example both strings and numbers have been assigned to the array elements. You can read back any value simply by referring to it, like this, which displays the value in `Occupation` (namely `Philanthropist`) in the browser:

```
document.write(MyInfo['Occupation'])
```

 In Lesson13 you will learn how JavaScript arrays are actually examples of objects (as are all JavaScript variables) and how they can be used in Object-Oriented Programming (OOP).

Summary

By now you should have a pretty good understanding of JavaScript arrays and should begin to see how they can make excellent structures for handling your data. In the following lesson I'll show you how there's actually a lot more to arrays than you've seen so far, and we'll begin to make some reasonably complex data objects.

Self-Test Questions

Test how much you have learned in this lesson with these questions. If you don't know an answer, go back and reread the relevant section until your knowledge is complete. You can find the answers in Appendix A.

1. Which characters are allowed as the first in an array name?

2. Which characters are allowed in the body of array names?

3. How would you create a new array called `mydata`?

4. How would you limit this new array to, for example, 20 elements?

5. How would you reference item 11 in the array `mydata`?

6. Is the first item in an array at index 0 or 1?

7. How can you populate an array with data at the time of creation?

8. What is an associative array?

9. How would you add the key/value pair of `Name`/`Alice` as a new element in the associative array `mydata`?

10. How would you retrieve the value for the key `Name` in the associative array `mydata`?

6

Accessing Multidimensional Arrays

 To view the accompanying video for this lesson, please visit mhprofessional.com/ nixonjavascript/.

Let me start by totally contradicting the title of this lesson and stating that there's actually no such thing as multidimensional arrays in JavaScript. But before you start scratching your head and wondering whether I've drunk too many cups of tea, let me say that you can *simulate* multidimensional arrays in JavaScript by assigning new arrays as the values for elements of an existing array.

But what exactly do I mean by *multidimensional* in the first place? Well, in the same way that a string of characters is a collection of individual letters, numbers, and other characters that you can imagine being like a string of pearls—with each pearl occupying its right location and the correct pearls on either side, all in the right order. An array, therefore, is like a collection of variables all stored in their right locations.

In the previous lesson I used the metaphor of a filing cabinet for an array of 10 elements. If you imagine for a moment that each drawer in this filing cabinet is like *Doctor Who*'s Tardis (his time and space machine) in that it is much bigger on the inside than it is on the outside, then you should be able to also imagine being able to place another 10-drawer filing cabinet in each of the drawers of the original one! Figure 6-1 should help make this clearer.

Remember that these particular filing cabinets are not bound by the normal rules of space and time, so the small cabinets can contain just as much as the large ones. In fact, the cabinets are capable of holding an infinite amount of data, limited only by the restraints of your browser, operating system, and available memory. I have simply drawn the secondary filing cabinets much smaller so that they fit into the figure.

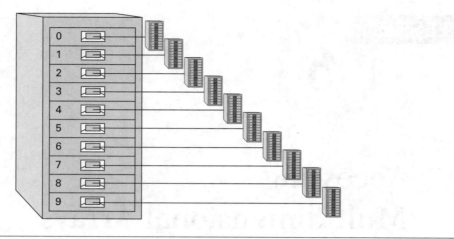

FIGURE 6-1   Representing a two-dimensional array with filing cabinets

Creating a Two-Dimensional Array

Let's see how we can use the ability of an array element to store another entire array to our advantage by considering a 10 times multiplication table, just like those often found on the walls of schools (see Figure 6-2).

	1	2	3	4	5	6	7	8	9	10
1	1	2	3	4	5	6	7	8	9	10
2	2	4	6	8	10	12	14	16	18	20
3	3	6	9	12	15	18	21	24	27	30
4	4	8	12	16	20	24	28	32	36	40
5	5	10	15	20	25	30	35	40	45	50
6	6	12	18	24	30	36	42	48	54	60
7	7	14	21	28	35	42	49	56	63	70
8	8	16	24	32	40	48	56	64	72	80
9	9	18	27	36	45	54	63	72	81	90
10	10	20	30	40	50	60	70	80	90	100

FIGURE 6-2   A 10 times multiplication table

Each of the columns (or each of the rows) can be considered a one-dimensional array. For example, the first row could be created using the following code:

```
MyTable0      = new Array()
MyTable0[0] = 1
MyTable1[1] = 2
MyTable2[2] = 3
MyTable3[3] = 4
MyTable4[4] = 5
MyTable5[5] = 6
MyTable6[6] = 7
MyTable7[7] = 8
MyTable8[8] = 9
MyTable9[9] = 10
```

Or, more succinctly:

```
MyTable0 = [1, 2, 3, 4, 5, 6, 7, 8, 9, 10]
```

Similarly, the second row could be created like this:

```
MyTable1 = [2, 4, 6, 8, 10, 12, 14, 16, 18, 20]
```

And so you can go on for rows 3 through 10, so that you end up with the following set of statements:

```
MyTable0 = [ 1,  2,  3,  4,  5,  6,  7,  8,  9, 10]
MyTable1 = [ 2,  4,  6,  8, 10, 12, 14, 16, 18, 20]
MyTable2 = [ 3,  6,  9, 12, 15, 18, 21, 24, 27, 30]
MyTable3 = [ 4,  8, 12, 16, 20, 24, 28, 32, 36, 40]
MyTable4 = [ 5, 10, 15, 20, 25, 30, 35, 40, 45, 50]
MyTable5 = [ 6, 12, 18, 24, 30, 36, 42, 48, 54, 60]
MyTable6 = [ 7, 14, 21, 28, 35, 42, 49, 56, 63, 70]
MyTable7 = [ 8, 16, 24, 32, 40, 48, 56, 64, 72, 80]
MyTable8 = [ 9, 18, 27, 36, 45, 54, 63, 72, 81, 90]
MyTable9 = [10, 20, 30, 40, 50, 60, 70, 80, 90,100]
```

At this point we now have 10 arrays—one for each row in the times table. With these now created, it is possible to build a two-dimensional table by creating just one more *master* table, like this:

```
MasterTable      = new Array()
MasterTable[0] = MyTable0
MasterTable[1] = MyTable1
MasterTable[2] = MyTable2
MasterTable[3] = MyTable3
MasterTable[4] = MyTable4
MasterTable[5] = MyTable5
MasterTable[6] = MyTable6
```

```
MasterTable[7] = MyTable7
MasterTable[8] = MyTable8
MasterTable[9] = MyTable9
```

Or by using the shorter form of:

```
MasterTable =
[
  MyTable0,
  MyTable1,
  MyTable2,
  MyTable3,
  MyTable4,
  MyTable5,
  MyTable6,
  MyTable7,
  MyTable8,
  MyTable9
]
```

 I have chosen to split this up into multiple lines for clarity, but you can equally include all the preceding in a single statement on one line.

Accessing a Two-Dimensional Array

Let's now look at how this relates to the filing cabinets in Figure 6-1 in terms of code. To recap, there is a main array called `MasterTable[]`, and its 10 elements each contain another array named `MyTable0[]` through `MyTable9[]`, as illustrated in Figure 6-3.

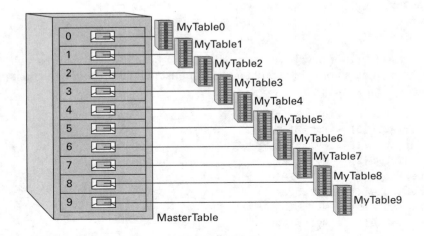

FIGURE 6-3   The relationship between the cabinets and arrays

As you will recall from Lesson 5, accessing an array is as simple as the following, which displays the value in the array held at a numeric index of 23 (which will be the 24th element because arrays start from 0) in an alert window:

```
alert(SomeArray[23])
```

But what should you do when the value stored in an array element is another array? The answer is simple and elegant—you simply add another pair of square brackets following the first pair and place an index value into that new array between them, like this:

```
alert(MasterTable[0][0])
```

This statement opens an alert window and displays in it the contents of the first element of the array that is stored in the first element of `MasterTable[]`. Notice that there is no need to reference the sub-array (*sub-array* being the term I use for referring to arrays within arrays) by name.

Likewise, if you wish to display the value held in the seventh element of the array stored in the third element of `MasterTable[]`, you would use code such as this (remembering that table indexes start at 0, not 1, so the seventh and third elements will be 6 and 2, respectively):

```
alert(MasterTable[2][6])
```

In terms of the times table in Figure 6-2, this is equivalent to first moving to the seventh column along and then down to the third row, at which point you can see that the value shown is 21, as you will quickly see if you look at the source of *timestable.htm* (available in the companion archive):

```
<!DOCTYPE html>
<html>
  <head>
    <title>Two-Dimensional Array Example</title>
  </head>
  <body>
    <script>
      MyTable0 = [ 1,  2,  3,  4,  5,  6,  7,  8,  9, 10]
      MyTable1 = [ 2,  4,  6,  8, 10, 12, 14, 16, 18, 20]
      MyTable2 = [ 3,  6,  9, 12, 15, 18, 21, 24, 27, 30]
      MyTable3 = [ 4,  8, 12, 16, 20, 24, 28, 32, 36, 40]
      MyTable4 = [ 5, 10, 15, 20, 25, 30, 35, 40, 45, 50]
      MyTable5 = [ 6, 12, 18, 24, 30, 36, 42, 48, 54, 60]
      MyTable6 = [ 7, 14, 21, 28, 35, 42, 49, 56, 63, 70]
      MyTable7 = [ 8, 16, 24, 32, 40, 48, 56, 64, 72, 80]
      MyTable8 = [ 9, 18, 27, 36, 45, 54, 63, 72, 81, 90]
      MyTable9 = [10, 20, 30, 40, 50, 60, 70, 80, 90,100]

      MasterTable = [MyTable0, MyTable1, MyTable2,
                     MyTable3, MyTable4, MyTable5,
```

```
                    MyTable6, MyTable7, MyTable8,
                    MyTable9]
       alert('The value at location 2,6 is ' + MasterTable[2][6])
     </script>
   </body>
 </html>
```

 This code is equivalent to the filing cabinets in Figure 6-1, in that the
`MasterTable[]` array represents the large cabinet, whereas the `MyTable0[]`
array is the top small cabinet and `MyTable9[]` is the bottom small cabinet,
as shown in Figure 6-3.

If you now take all these small filing cabinets and stack them up alongside each
other, you will now see how they represent the `MasterTable[]` array, as shown in
Figure 6-4. For all intents and purposes, we can forget about the main array (other
than using its name to index into the sub-arrays), think only in terms of the 10 sub-
arrays and how to access each drawer using pairs of indexes.

FIGURE 6-4   The small filing cabinets are now lined up alongside each other.

The first index goes along the cabinets from left to right (equivalent to going
from the top to bottom drawer of `MasterTable[]`, because each of these cabinets
in order is in the next drawer down of `MasterTable[]`), and the second one goes
from the top to the bottom drawer of each cabinet. Therefore, array index `[3][7]`
points to the fourth filing cabinet along and the eighth drawer down. In other words,
`MasterTable[3][7]` refers to the value held in the eighth drawer down of the
fourth cabinet along.

A More Practical Example

Obviously, a multiplication table is a trivial thing to re-create on a computer, as it
can be achieved with a couple of simple loops. Therefore, let's look instead at a more
practical example: that of a board for a game of chess.

As you likely know, there are 64 squares on a chessboard, laid out in an 8 × 8 grid,
and there are two sets of 16 pieces: black and white. Using a computer to represent
a chessboard in its starting position and ignoring the fact that the squares alternate

between dark and light, you might use code such as this (in which uppercase letters represent white pieces, and the lowercase ones are black):

```
Row0 = ['r', 'n', 'b', 'q', 'k', 'b', 'n', 'r']
Row1 = ['p', 'p', 'p', 'p', 'p', 'p', 'p', 'p']
Row2 = ['-', '-', '-', '-', '-', '-', '-', '-']
Row3 = ['-', '-', '-', '-', '-', '-', '-', '-']
Row4 = ['-', '-', '-', '-', '-', '-', '-', '-']
Row5 = ['-', '-', '-', '-', '-', '-', '-', '-']
Row6 = ['P', 'P', 'P', 'P', 'P', 'P', 'P', 'P']
Row7 = ['R', 'N', 'B', 'Q', 'K', 'B', 'N', 'R']
```

The dashes represent locations where there is no chess piece, and the key for the other letters is as follows:

- R/r Rooks
- N/n Knights
- B/b Bishops
- Q/q Queens
- K/k Kings
- P/p Pawns

You can now insert all these arrays into a master array that holds the complete chessboard, like this:

```
Board = [Row0, Row1, Row2, Row3, Row4, Row5, Row6, Row7]
```

Now we are ready to move pieces about on the board. Therefore, for example, let's assume that the white player opens with the standard *pawn to king 4* move. Using the array notation of locations [0][0] through [7][7], with [0][0] being the top left corner, and [7][7] the bottom right, this is equivalent to setting the location [6][4] to '-' to remove the pawn currently at this location, and then setting [4][4] to P to place the pawn in its new position. In terms of code, it would look like this:

```
Temp        = Board[6][4]
Board[6][4] = '-'
Board[4][4] = Temp
```

In this example a new variable called Temp is used to store the value extracted from Board[6][4]. Then Board[6][4] is set to a dash character to remove the piece, and the value now in Temp is then placed into Board[4][4], overwriting whatever value it previously held.

Or, if it's not necessary to hold a copy of the piece being moved (which it is not in this very simple simulation), then you can simply set the two array locations to their required values, like this:

```
Board[6][4] = '-'
Board[4][4] = 'P'
```

Figure 6-5 shows the *chess.htm* example file (available in the companion archive), in which the before- and after-board positions are shown, as created by the preceding code.

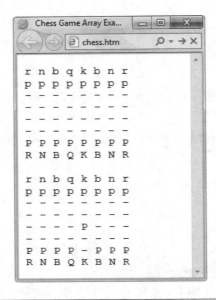

FIGURE 6-5   Moves resulting from modifying a two-dimensional chessboard array

 If you wish, you may continue adding arrays within other arrays until you run out of computer memory. All you do is place new arrays inside existing ones to add an extra dimension. For example, if you were to create an additional 8 sub–sub-arrays for each of the sub-array elements (a total of 64 new arrays), you would form eight complete chessboards in a three-dimensional array, representing an 8 × 8 × 8 cube—3D chess anyone?

Multidimensional Associative Arrays

As you might expect, as with numeric arrays, you can create multidimensional associative arrays. Let me explain why you might want to do this by considering a small online store that sells toys for the following six different age ranges of children:

- Babies
- Toddlers
- Age 3–5
- Age 5–8
- Age 8–12
- Teenagers

These categories can be easily mapped into an associative array, as I show you in a minute. But let's first create some subcategories for each of the main ones, such as these:

- Babies
  - Rattle
  - Bear
  - Pacifier
- Toddlers
  - Wooden Bricks
  - Xylophone
  - Play-Doh
- Age 3–5
  - Slide
  - Tricycle
  - Crayons
- Age 5–8
  - Dolly
  - Bicycle
  - Guitar
- Age 8–12
  - Tablet Computer
  - Remote-Control Car
  - Frisbee
- Teenagers
  - MP3 Player
  - Game Console
  - TV/DVD Combo

Clearly these subcategories can also be mapped to associative arrays, but before we do that, we have to go even deeper (yet more undertones of *Inception*) because a web store needs things such as pricing information and product availability, like this:

- Price
- Stock Level

Creating the Multidimensional Array

Armed with these details, we're now ready to start building the arrays needed by assigning values to the price and stock level of each product being sold to a two-dimensional array for each product, as follows:

```
Rattle    = { 'Price' :   4.99, 'Stock' : 3 }
Bear      = { 'Price' :   6.99, 'Stock' : 2 }
Pacifier  = { 'Price' :   1.99, 'Stock' : 9 }
```

```
Bricks    = { 'Price' :   5.99, 'Stock' : 1 }
Xylophone = { 'Price' :  12.99, 'Stock' : 2 }
Play-Doh  = { 'Price' :   8.49, 'Stock' : 7 }
Slide     = { 'Price' :  99.99, 'Stock' : 1 }
Tricycle  = { 'Price' :  79.99, 'Stock' : 1 }
Crayons   = { 'Price' :   3.79, 'Stock' : 5 }
Dolly     = { 'Price' :  14.99, 'Stock' : 3 }
Bicycle   = { 'Price' :  89.99, 'Stock' : 2 }
Guitar    = { 'Price' :  49.00, 'Stock' : 1 }
TabletPC  = { 'Price' : 149.99, 'Stock' : 1 }
RemoteCar = { 'Price' :  39.99, 'Stock' : 2 }
Frisbee   = { 'Price' :   7.99, 'Stock' : 6 }
MP3Player = { 'Price' : 179.99, 'Stock' : 1 }
Console   = { 'Price' : 199.99, 'Stock' : 2 }
TVAndDVD  = { 'Price' :  99.99, 'Stock' : 1 }
```

Now that these basic data structures are complete, it's possible to group the products into the age range arrays, like this (where the words in quotes are the keys and those after the colons are the values, which are the names of the arrays previously created):

```
Babies    = { 'Rattle'                : Rattle,
              'Bear'                  : Bear,
              'Pacifier'              : Pacifier }
Toddlers  = { 'Wooden Bricks'         : Bricks,
              'Xylophone'             : Xylophone,
              'Play Dough'            : Play-Doh }
Age3_5    = { 'Slide'                 : Slide,
              'Tricycle'              : Tricycle,
              'Crayons'               : Crayons }
Age5_8    = { 'Dolly'                 : Dolly,
              'Bicycle'               : Bicycle,
              'Guitar'                : Guitar }
Age8_12   = { 'Tablet PC'             : TabletPC,
              'Remote Control Car'    : RemoteCar,
              'Frisbee'               : Frisbee }
Teenagers = { 'MP3 Player'            : MP3Player,
              'Game Console'          : Console,
              'TV/DVD Combo'          : TVAndDVD }
```

 I used an underline character between the digits in these age range arrays because the dash is a disallowed character in variable or array names (because it can be confused with the minus symbol). The dash is acceptable, however, when used as part of a quoted string for a key name.

And finally the top array can be populated, like this (where the strings in quotes are the keys, and the values after the colons are the names of the arrays just defined):

```
Categories = { 'Toddlers'   : Toddlers,
               'Ages 3-5'   : Age3_5,
               'Ages 5-8'   : Age5_8,
               'Ages 8-12'  : Age8_12,
               'Teenagers'  : Teenagers }
```

What has now been created is actually a three-dimensional array. The first dimension is the Categories[] array, the second is each of the age range arrays, and the third is each of the product arrays containing the price and stock level.

 Remember that in each of these assignments the string on the left is the key and the item on the right is the value. In all but the innermost (or lowest) case, the value is the name of another array that has already been created. For the innermost case, the values are numeric values: the price and stock level.

Accessing the Arrays

You can now read and write to these stored values in the following manner, which returns the price of the slide, which is 99.99 (no currency type is specified in these examples, just values):

```
document.write(Categories['Ages 3-5']['Slide']['Price'])
```

Or, if you need to change a price on an item of inventory for any reason, such as the crayons (currently 3.79), you can alter it in the following manner, which reduces the price by 0.20:

```
Categories['Ages 3-5']['Crayons']['Price'] = 3.59
```

Likewise, when you sell an item of stock, you can reduce the inventory level (the stock level) in a similar manner, such as the following, which decreases the stock level of game consoles by 1 using the pre-decrement operator:

```
--Categories['Teenagers']['Game Console']['Stock']
```

Obviously, the inventory for even the smallest online store is sure to be far greater than in this example, and there are going to be many additional attributes for some toys, such as different sizes and colors and even any images, descriptions, and technical specifications or other details about the product that are available, all of which could easily be built into this multidimensional structure of arrays.

The file *toystore.htm* in the companion archive contains all the preceding pre-populated arrays and the example statements that access them. You may wish to try experimenting with it to read from and write to other items of data within the array structure.

The actual job of storing all your data will take place on a web server in a secure environment tightly controlled by your database management system. The purpose of using a structure of arrays in JavaScript like this, therefore, is purely for you to support easy manipulation of data for users within their browsers as they view your merchandise, without them having to leave your page, or transfer any data to or from the web server until an item is added to the user's shopping cart.

Summary

Believe it or not, we've actually covered a huge amount of territory in just six lessons. Hopefully it's all making sense to you, and arrays are beginning to feel like second nature. With this full understanding of how arrays are created and manipulated in JavaScript, in Lesson 7 we'll look at some fun we can have using its array-accessing functions.

Self-Test Questions

Test how much you have learned in this lesson with these questions. If you don't know an answer, go back and reread the relevant section until your knowledge is complete. You can find the answers in Appendix A.

1. How can you create a multidimensional array?

2. How do you access a two-dimensional numeric array?

3. How do you access a two-dimensional associative array?

4. How many levels deep can you nest additional arrays within a master array?

5. How might you construct a multidimensional array for a class of 30 history students to hold their grades for a year's two semesters?

6. How might you extend this array to handle four years' worth of semesters?

7. In the chessboard example, what code would represent the black player responding by moving *pawn to queen 4*?

8. And what code might represent the white player's *pawn at king 4* taking the black player's pawn?

9. What would you do to turn a three-dimensional chessboard array into a four-dimensional array?

10. In the final example, what single line of code would increment the stock of toddlers' bricks by 12?

Calling Array Functions

 To view the accompanying video for this lesson, please visit mhprofessional.com/ nixonjavascript/.

To make arrays even more powerful, JavaScript comes ready-made with a selection of handy functions and statements for accessing and manipulating arrays. For example, you can join arrays together, push new items into an array (and pop them off again later), reverse the data in an array, sort it alphabetically or numerically, and more.

Therefore, in this and the following couple of lessons, we'll look at these functions and how to use them.

Using `for (... in ...)`

The first feature I'd like to introduce is `for (... in ...)`, because with it you can iterate through an array one element at a time, which we will need to do in the following examples in order to see the results. To show how this iteration works, let's start with a simple array of cat types:

```
Cats = [ 'Long Hair',
         'Short Hair',
         'Dwarf',
         'Farm',
         'Tabby',
         'Tortoiseshell' ]
```

Now, let's use for (... in ...) to display all its elements, as follows (resulting in Figure 7-1):

```
for (index in Cats)
{
  document.write(Cats[index] + '<br>')
}
```

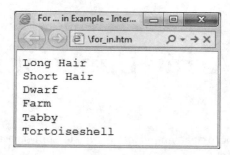

FIGURE 7-1   The contents of **Cats** is displayed.

What's happening here is the for() keyword creates a new variable called index, which it initializes with the integer value of 0, so that it points to the first element in the array specified (in this case Cats[]).

Then the contents of the curly braces are executed once for each element in the Cats[] array, with index being incremented each time around. Therefore, the first time element 0 is indexed by index, the second time, it is element 1, and so on until there are no more elements left in the array to process.

For reasons I explain in Lesson 10, the curly braces can be omitted when there is only a single statement to be executed by such a for() loop. Therefore, for the sake of simplicity in the following examples, I will reduce this type of code to the much shorter example (which also uses the index variable i instead of index but is equally valid syntax):

```
for (i in Cats) document.write(Cats[i] + '<br>')
```

Now that there's an easy way to display the contents of an array, we can start to look at the array functions provided by JavaScript and see how to use them. You can try this example yourself by loading the *for_in.htm* example from the companion archive into your browser.

Using concat()

Using the concat() function, you can return a new array created by joining two other arrays together. The two original arrays are not changed in any way by this function; only the result of joining them together is returned.

To see how this works, let's create a second array to go with the `Cats[]` array created a little earlier, as follows:

```
Dogs = [ 'Pit Bull',
         'Spaniel',
         'Terrier',
         'Beagle',
         'Shepherd',
         'Bulldog' ]
```

With both arrays now created, we can run the `concat()` function on them, like this:

```
Pets = Cats.concat(Dogs)
```

And now to see the result of this operation, we can issue the following statement:

```
for (i in Pets) document.write(Pets[i] + '<br>')
```

The code to create these two arrays and the preceding pair of statements are in the *concat.htm* file in the companion archive. As you can see in Figure 7-2, the result is that the new array `Pets[]` now contains all elements from both the `Cats[]` and `Dogs[]` arrays, in order.

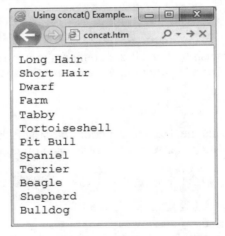

FIGURE 7-2   The two arrays have been concatenated.

For a similar result, but with the contents of the `Dogs[]` array before the `Cats[]`, you could have issued this statement:

```
Pets = Dogs.concat(Cats)
```

In fact, you could omit the creation of the `Pets[]` array altogether and simply iterate through the result of the `concat()` call, like this:

```
for (i in Dogs.concat(Cats))
   document.write(Dogs.concat(Cats)[i] + '<br>')
```

Although it works, the preceding is wasteful code because the `concat()` function has ended up being used twice and called multiple times in the loop. Because the result of the concatenation is lost once you have accessed it, this isn't recommended coding practice. However, this code illustrates that by placing square brackets containing an index variable after the call to `concat()` (namely `[i]`), you can index into the array returned by the call.

An Alternative to `concat()`

If all you want to do is quickly see what values are in an array, you can use the implied concatenation you get when referencing an array as an argument to the document `.write()` function. For example, you can list all the elements in the `Dogs[]` array to the browser (separated with commas), like this:

```
document.write(Dogs)
```

Note how you must omit the `[]` characters from after the array name in order for this to work, and the result of this statement will then be like the following:

```
Pit Bull,Spaniel,Terrier,Beagle,Shepherd,Bulldog
```

Using `join()`

Sometimes you may wish to turn all the elements in an array into a string, and this is easy to do using the `join()` function. For example, let's take the following case of the `Cats[]` array:

```
document.write(Cats.join(' and '))
```

This statement calls the `join()` function, passing it the string `' and '`, which is used as a separator, which is inserted between each element, as shown in Figure 7-3.

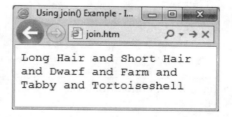

FIGURE 7-3   The result of joining array elements into a string

You may use any string as the element separator, or none at all, as in the following three examples (with extra spaces inserted to clearly show what's going on):

```
document.write(Cats.join(', ') + '<br>')
document.write(Cats.join(''  ) + '<br>')
document.write(Cats.join(     )             )
```

When no argument is passed to `join()`, a comma is assumed as the separator, whereas to have no separator, you should supply an empty string (`' '`). Therefore, in turn, the three previous statements display the following:

```
Long Hair, Short Hair, Dwarf, Farm, Tabby, Tortoiseshell
Long HairShort HairDwarfFarmTabbyTortoiseshell
Long Hair,Short Hair,Dwarf,Farm,Tabby,Tortoiseshell
```

The `forEach()` Function

An alternative to using `for (... in ...)` is the `forEach()` function. With it, you can iterate through an array of elements very easily, as follows (where v in the arguments of the `Info()` function is the value of each element, i is the index of the element, and a is the array being traversed, which is `Dogs[]` in this case):

```
Dogs = [ 'Pit Bull',
         'Spaniel',
         'Terrier',
         'Beagle',
         'Shepherd',
         'Bulldog' ]

Dogs.forEach(Info)

function Info(v, i, a)
{
   document.write('[' + i + '] is ' + v + '<br>')
}
```

As shown in Figure 7-4, the `Info()` function simply displays information about each element in the array. The powerful thing is that the `forEach()` function name is simply attached to the `Dogs[]` array name with a period operator, and (without needing any loops) the array gets processed by the `Info()` function, which has been passed as the argument to `forEach()`.

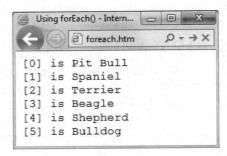

FIGURE 7-4   Iterating through an array with **`forEach()`**

The `map()` Function

One very quick and easy way to process all the elements in an array is to pass each element in the array to a function via JavaScript's `map()` function. For example, the following code creates an array populated with numbers, and then applies the `Math.sqrt()` function to each element, returning the results in the new array `Roots[]`, all via a single call to the `map()` function.

```
Nums  = [99, 16, 11, 66.5, 54, 23]
Roots = Nums.map(Math.sqrt)
```

You can see the result of running this code (*maps.htm* in the companion archive) in Figure 7-5.

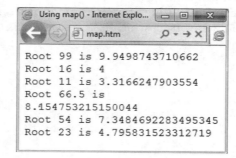

FIGURE 7-5   Applying the `map()` function to an array

Summary

In this lesson you have learned how to process arrays to extract data from them in loops, how to apply a function to them and to individual elements, and how to join arrays together. Therefore, now you will be able to use arrays for complex data storage and manipulation. In the following lesson we'll look at how you can also use arrays for temporary data storage in the form of stacks to support advanced techniques such as recursion.

Self-Test Questions

Using these questions, test how much you have learned in this lesson If you don't know an answer, go back and reread the relevant section until your knowledge is complete. You can find the answers in Appendix A.

1. How can you use the `for (... in ...)` function to iterate through an array one element at a time?

2. Which function is similar to using `for (... in ...)`, but can be implemented with a single instruction?

3. With which function can you join two arrays together into a single array?

4. What single line of code would you use to join together two arrays called `tennis[]` and `golf[]` into a third called `sports[]`?

5. How can you quickly pass an entire array of elements to a function?

6. With a single line of code, how can you easily invoke a function on each element of an array and return a new array containing the processed element values?

7. What is the `join()` function used for?

8. What single line of code would you use to display all the elements in the array `sports[]` as a string, with each separated from the next by the string ' plus '?

9. If you have an array of hobby names called `hobbies`, what does the command `document.write(hobbies)` do?

10. What does the command `activities = sports.concat(hobbies)` do?

PART II

Advanced
JavaScript

Pushing to and Popping from Arrays

 To view the accompanying video for this lesson, please visit mhprofessional.com/ nixonjavascript/.

In addition to assigning values to an array when you create it or adding those values using numeric indexes or associative keys, you can simply push items of data onto an array and pop them off later. When doing this, you don't need to keep track of an index number or any key names; you simply push a value and forget about it until you want to pop it back off the array later.

This makes it very easy to store certain types of temporary data suited to being held in what is known as a stack, a data storage structure that is so important that it is even implemented in the core of every microprocessor chip to aid with processing instructions in the right order.

In this lesson you learn how to use different types of stacks to achieve some useful data manipulation results.

Using push()

There are a couple of good reasons for using the push() function. First, you can add a new element to the end of an array without knowing how many items already exist in that array. For example, normally you would need to know the current array length and then use that value to add extra values, like this (using the Cats array from Lesson 7 once more):

```
Cats = [ 'Long Hair',
         'Short Hair',
         'Dwarf',
```

```
            'Farm',
            'Tabby',
            'Tortoiseshell' ]

len         = Cats.length
Cats[len]   = "Siamese"
```

The new variable `len` is used to hold the length of the array (the number of elements it contains). In this instance the value will be 6 (for elements 0 through 5). Therefore, the value in `len`, being 6, is suitable as an index into the next available element, and so that is what it is used for—the value 6 pointing to the seventh element (because array indexes start at 0).

In fact, if the variable `len` is not to be used anywhere else, it is actually superfluous, because you could replace the final two lines of the preceding example with this single statement:

```
Cats[Cats.length] = "Siamese"
```

However, for certain purposes it can be much simpler to let JavaScript keep track of array lengths and simply tell it to add a new element to the `Cats` array, like this:

```
Cats.push('Siamese')
```

You can verify that the element has been added with the following `for ()` loop (which results in Figure 8-1, the code for which is available as *push.htm* in the companion archive):

```
for (i in Cats) document.write(Cats[i] + '<br>')
```

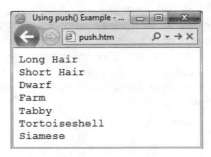

FIGURE 8-1   Pushing an element onto an array

The second reason you might want to use `Push ()` is that it is a quick way of storing values in a sequence that then have to be recalled in the reverse order. For example, using `push()`, you can keep adding elements to an array, like this:

```
MyArray.push('A')
MyArray.push('B')
MyArray.push('C')
```

Then, as you will see in the following description of pop(), you can also remove these elements from last to first, such that the value C will be taken off first, then B, then A, and so on.

Using pop()

At its simplest, pop() enables you to remove the last element from an array (and in this instance discard the returned value), using code such as this:

```
MyArray.pop()
```

Or, to remove the last element from an array and store it in a variable (for example), you use code such as this:

```
MyVariable = MyArray.pop()
```

You can apply pop() to an existing array with values in, which may have been assigned when the array was created, via a call to push() or in any other way. The pop() function then pulls the last item off the array (removing it from the array) and then returns that value. Considering the Cats array, a working example might look like this:

```
Cats = [ 'Long Hair',
         'Short Hair',
         'Dwarf',
         'Farm',
         'Tabby',
         'Tortoiseshell' ]
document.write('Popping off the value ' + Cats.pop() + '<br><br>')

document.write('Remaining elements: <br><br>')
for (i in Cats) document.write(Cats[i] + '<br>')
```

The result of running this code (available as *pop.htm* in the companion archive) is shown in Figure 8-2, where you can see that the value Tortoiseshell was popped off the array and underneath all the remaining elements are displayed—confirming that the previous final element has now been removed.

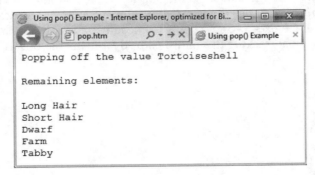

FIGURE 8-2   Popping an element off an array

Using push() and pop() Together

The pop() function is most commonly used with push() when writing code that uses *recursion*. Recursion is any section of code that calls itself and can then call itself again, and keep on doing so until the task of the code is complete (it's like *Inception* yet again!).

If this sounds complicated, consider a search algorithm for exploring a maze such as the one in Figure 8-3, in which the objective is to find your way from the starting point at a to the finish at y.

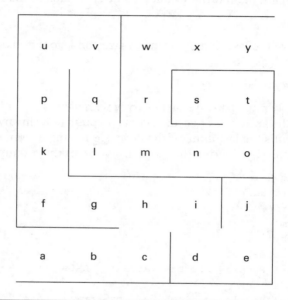

FIGURE 8-3   A simple 5 × 5 maze

You can clearly see the path to follow, but a computer is not so smart and will need to investigate the maze as if it were a rat, with walls higher than it can see over. Therefore, a program to do this will easily find its way along the path a-b-c-h, but then it will encounter a choice of going either left to location (or cell) g, or right to i.

Let's assume it chooses the latter after selecting a direction at random. The program will then follow the path i-d-e-j, only to encounter a dead end, requiring the program to return. Let's look at tracking this entire path so far using the push() function:

```
Maze = new Array()
Maze.push('a')
Maze.push('b')
Maze.push('c')
Maze.push('h')
Maze.push('i')
Maze.push('d')
Maze.push('e')
Maze.push('j')
```

If you assume that there's also some extra code (not documented here) that knows which cells the program has and hasn't yet visited, it can now use the simple method of popping each cell off the array until it reaches one where it can get to a cell not yet visited. Pseudo-code (the actions to take expressed in plain English) to do this might look as follows:

```
While no unvisited cell is accessible
  pop a location off the array
```

And the sequence of actions that would happen within the loop section of this code would be like this:

```
Location = Maze.pop() // Returns 'j'
```

Because no unvisited cell can be reached from j (as determined by the code that we assume is there but not documented), the loop will go around again and again until an unvisited cell can be accessed, resulting in four additional calls to pop(), as follows:

```
Location = Maze.pop() // Returns 'e'
Location = Maze.pop() // Returns 'd'
Location = Maze.pop() // Returns 'i'
Location = Maze.pop() // Returns 'h'
```

Now, when the program finds it has popped the location h off the stack, it discovers there is a new cell it can go to, namely g, and so the process continues along the path g-f-k-p-u-v-q-l-m, at which point another choice of directions is encountered: either r or n.

To track this path, the program will push all the cells between g and m onto the array, and then (if it continues straight ahead) also push the path n-o-t-s, at which point another dead end is encountered.

Then, as before, the code pops off all the cells in a loop until it reaches m, at which point the unvisited cell r is accessible and the final path out of the maze is discovered: r-w-x-y.

Note Recursion is quite complex programming, especially for beginners, which is why I have not documented the ancillary code you would use to take care of tracking the visited and unvisited cells. I simply wanted to offer a visual example of recursion that would explain what's going on and show you how to use push() and pop() together. But don't worry if you find any of it confusing, as you can safely move on with the book and come back here another time when you find an actual need for these functions.

Using reverse()

When you want to reverse the order of elements in an array, you can call the reverse() function, which actually reverses the array contents, rather than returning a new array as some other functions do.

To use the function, simply attach it to the array to be reversed, like this:

```
MyArray.reverse()
```

Figure 8-4 shows this function being used to reverse the `Cats` array from earlier in this lesson, the code for which is available as *reverse.htm* in the companion archive.

FIGURE 8-4 Array elements before and after reversing

Using Stacks and Buffers

The `reverse()` function is sometimes used on an array of elements that have been created by pushing the values onto it. As you will know from the earlier `push()` section, pushed values are added to the end of an array such that when you come to pop them off again, they are returned in reverse order. This is often referred to as a FILO (First In/Last Out) or sometimes as a LIFO (Last In/First Out) array. When an array is used this way, it is also sometimes called a *stack*.

But if you wish to operate a FIFO (First In/First Out) or LILO (Last In/Last Out) array—both are the same thing—you can reverse an array before pushing an item onto it and then reverse it again, ready for elements to be popped off. That way, the first value pushed onto it will be the first one popped off, and so on.

This type of array is also known as a *buffer*, and is typically used for handling events such as keyboard input, in which the key presses should be stored (buffered) until needed and returned in the order they were pressed.

Buffering Using an Array

You can see a simulation of this in the following code, in which the word Fred is being pushed into the array Buffer() as if entered one key press at a time, with the array's contents shown in the comment immediately following each statement. The top (or start) of the array is at the left of the string shown in the comments, and the bottom (or end) of the array (onto which values are pushed and popped) is at the right of the string:

```
Buffer.reverse() // Buffer = ''
Buffer.push('F') // Buffer = 'F'
Buffer.reverse() // Buffer = 'F'

Buffer.reverse() // Buffer = 'F'
Buffer.push('r') // Buffer = 'Fr'
Buffer.reverse() // Buffer = 'rF'

Buffer.reverse() // Buffer = 'Fr'
Buffer.push('e') // Buffer = 'Fre'
Buffer.reverse() // Buffer = 'erF'

Buffer.reverse() // Buffer = 'Fre'
Buffer.push('d') // Buffer = 'Fred'
Buffer.reverse() // Buffer = 'derF'
```

Initially, Buffer() is empty and has no elements, but then the letter F is pushed onto it. Seeing as the array has only a single element; reversing it at this point has no effect. However, when the next letter r is to be added, it is pushed to the bottom of the array, denoted in the comment as being on the right of the F.

After the array is reversed back again, the r is at the top and F is at the bottom of the array. This is exactly where we want these elements to be, because if the code that uses this buffering system is ready to process the next key press in the buffer, it can simply issue a call to pop(), which will pull the letter F off it. This is correct because when processing buffered data such as this, the letters typed must be processed in the order typed.

When the letter e is processed, the array is once again reversed so that the new letter can be added to the bottom of the array. Then the array is reversed back again so that if pop() is called at *this* point, F will be the first letter popped off. After this third set of statements, F is at the bottom of the array, r is in the middle, and e is at the top.

Finally, the letter d is processed using the same procedure so that after it has been placed in the array, it is at the top, with the F at the bottom.

You can now retrieve this keyboard input from the array, using the pop() function as many times as required (in this instance, four times), like this:

```
KeyPress = Buffer.pop()
```

Creating a Function for Pushing to the Top

If you need a way to push values to the start of an array (instead of the end), you can create a `PushToTop()` function, using `push()` in conjunction with `reverse()`:

```
function PushToTop(Object, value)
{
  Object.reverse()
  Object.push(value)
  Object.reverse()
}
```

Then you simply call the new function, instead of each group of three statements in the previous example, like this:

```
PushToTop(Buffer, 'F')
PushToTop(Buffer, 'r')
PushToTop(Buffer, 'e')
PushToTop(Buffer, 'd')
```

Then, to retrieve the key presses in the right order, you simply call `pop()` as many times as necessary, like this:

```
KeyPress = Buffer.pop()
```

 Lesson 12 explains in detail how to write functions, pass values to them, and return values back to the calling code.

The `shift()` and `unshift()` Functions

Actually, JavaScript *does* have a built-in function to push to the other end of an array—I simply wanted to show how you could combine `reverse()` and `push()` to achieve the same result. But you can, in fact, push values to the top of an array, using the (curiously named) `unshift()` function. Likewise, you can also pop from the top of an array, using the `shift()` function. Therefore, the following code is all you would need to replicate the preceding examples:

```
Buffer.unshift('F')
Buffer.unshift('r')
Buffer.unshift('e')
Buffer.unshift('d')
```

Then, to retrieve these values in the order they were saved, you would simply use the `pop()` function to fetch first F, then r, e, and d, like this:

```
KeyPress = Buffer.pop()
```

However, because the `shift()` function retrieves from the other end of the array to `pop()`, we can also turn the whole code on its head and go back to using the following code to populate the array:

```
Buffer.push('F')
Buffer.push('r')
Buffer.push('e')
Buffer.push('d')
```

And then, to treat the array `Buffer` as an actual buffer (not a stack), just use `shift()` to retrieve these values in the order in which they were pushed onto the array (F, r, e, and finally d), like this:

```
KeyPress = Buffer.shift()
```

Summary

Using the functions covered in this lesson, your ability to manipulate data in arrays has taken a quantum leap and you will now be able to handle even the most sophisticated of data structures. In the following (and final) lesson on arrays, we'll take things one stage further by delving right into their insides and splicing in and out whole sections of arrays.

Self-Test Questions

Using these questions, test how much you have learned in this lesson. If you don't know an answer, go back and reread the relevant section until your knowledge is complete. You can find the answers in Appendix A.

1. Which function adds a new element to the bottom of an array?

2. Which function removes an element from the bottom of an array?

3. Which function adds a new element to the top of an array?

4. Which function removes an element from the top of an array?

5. What is a First In/Last Out (FILO) array also known as?

6. What is a First In/First Out (FIFO) array also known as?

7. With which function can you invert the order of elements in an array?

8. How can you determine the number of elements in an array?

9. What is the name given to the process of a section of code repeatedly calling itself?

10. Which array structure (stack or buffer) is best suited for the programming type described in Question 9?

Advanced Array Manipulation

 To view the accompanying video for this lesson, please visit mhprofessional.com/ nixonjavascript/.

In this final lesson on JavaScript arrays, we finish off our exploration by looking at how to sort the contents of arrays in a variety of different ways and how to manipulate groups of elements within arrays, including removing, inserting, and moving them.

Using `sort()`

JavaScript comes with a handy `sort()` function to sort arrays alphabetically in ascending order with case sensitivity. Like `reverse()`, this function changes the actual array to which it is applied, unlike some other functions that simply return a new array, leaving the original untouched.

To sort an array, simply call the `sort()` function on the array, as with this example that uses the `Cats` array:

```
Cats = [ 'Long Hair',
        'Short Hair',
        'Dwarf',
        'Farm',
        'Tabby',
        'Tortoiseshell' ]

Cats.sort()
```

The result of issuing this `sort()` call (the code for which is available as *sort.htm* in the companion archive) is shown in Figure 9-1.

FIGURE 9-1   Sorting an array alphabetically

Tailoring the `sort()` Function

If all you require is a case-sensitive alphabetical sort in ascending order, `sort()` is just the function for you. However, should you need to sort in reverse order or sort an array numerically, you need to provide some extra code to `sort()` to help it achieve this.

 Enhancing the `sort()` function requires using functions that you will write, so because I don't properly cover functions until Lesson 12, if the following makes you scratch your head, remember that you can simply copy and paste the code and it will work anyway, without you having to know (yet) just how it works.

Sorting Numerically

When an alphabetical sort is used, numbers are treated as strings so that, for example, the number 200 will come before the number 3 (because 2 comes before 3). In order to sort an array numerically, you must pass a helper function to the `sort()` function. This helper needs to tell `sort()` how to compare pairs of items as it sorts. Therefore, to sort an array numerically in ascending order, you can supply a function such as this:

```
function SortNumeric(a, b)
{
  return a - b
}
```

What this function does is accept two array elements (for example, it might be elements 0 and 1) and then it tests whether the first element is greater than the second by subtracting the second from the first.

If the result of this subtraction is greater than 0, b is smaller than a. Or, if it's less than 0, b is greater than a; otherwise, they have the same value. Therefore, what gets returned by SortNumeric() is either a negative, a zero, or a positive value, from which the sort() function decides the order in which to place the two elements, as follows:

- If the result returned by SortNumeric() is negative, b is greater than a, and therefore the element represented by a must appear before the one represented by b.
- If the result is positive, b is smaller than a, and so the element represented by b must appear before that represented by a.
- If the values in a and b are equal, there is no need to change the positions of the elements represented by a and b, so nothing happens.

The SortNumeric() function is passed to the sort() function, like this:

```
Numbers = [7, 62, 3, 99, 74, 11, 16, 1]
Numbers.sort(SortNumeric)
```

The first statement creates the array Numbers, in which a variety of different numeric values are stored. Then the second statement calls the sort() function on that array, passing it the name of the helper function to use (namely SortNumeric), but omitting the parentheses that usually follow a function name.

This is because we are telling sort() which function to use and not passing it the result of calling the function (more on this in the following lesson). The result of running this code is shown in Figure 9-2.

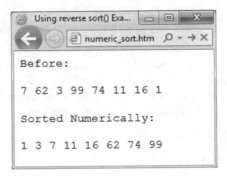

FIGURE 9-2   Sorting an array numerically

At the expense of readability, if you wish, you can bypass the requirement for creating a function to perform the sort by including an inline anonymous (unnamed) function as the argument to the sort() function instead, as with the following example that sorts the Numbers array numerically in ascending order:

```
Numbers.sort(function(a, b) { return a - b })
```

Reversing a Sort

To obtain a reversed sort of any kind, all you need to do is pass the sorted array to the reverse() function, like this (as shown in Figure 9-3):

```
Cats.sort().reverse()
```

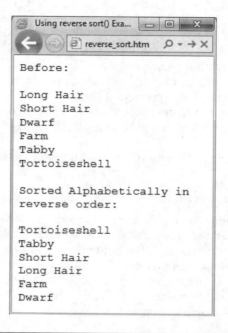

FIGURE 9-3   Reversing a sorted array

 You will probably have realized that for numeric arrays the expression `return a - b` in the `SortNumeric()` function could be replaced with `return b - a`, which would also result in a reversed sort—one example of how you can achieve the same outcome in JavaScript using different methods.

Using `splice()`

I've left possibly the most powerful array function, `splice()`, until last—not just because it comes last alphabetically, but because you can use it to provide the same facility as most of the other array functions, and a lot more too.

With `splice()` you can remove one or more elements from an array, or insert one or more into an array, and you can do either at any position within the array. What's more, you can remove and insert at the same time, providing a replace facility that can swap one or more elements with more, the same, or fewer elements.

Removing Elements from an Array

Let's look first at how to remove one or more elements from an array, starting with the `Cats` array we've been using a lot. In the following example, the `splice()` function is called with two arguments. The first is the element at which to perform the splice (starting from 0), and the second is the number of elements to be removed:

```
Cats = [ 'Long Hair',
         'Short Hair',
         'Dwarf',
         'Farm',
         'Tabby',
         'Tortoiseshell' ]

Cats.splice(2, 3)
```

Therefore, with arguments of 2 and 3, the splice starts at the element index 2, which is the third element, and the second argument of 3 states that three elements are to be removed from the array. If you need to know which elements have been removed, you can access the result of calling the function, which is an array containing the removed elements, like this:

```
Removed = Cats.splice(2, 3)
```

Figure 9-4 shows this code brought together, displaying the array before splicing, the elements removed by the splice, and the elements remaining afterward.

FIGURE 9-4   Removing elements from an array

Inserting Elements into an Array

Using a similar call to `splice()`, you can insert new values into the array, as in the following example, which adds two more breeds of cat starting at the third element:

```
Cats.splice(2, 0, 'Siamese', 'Persian')
```

Here, the first argument of 2 is the third element in the array, and the second argument of 0 tells `splice()` that there are no elements to be removed. After this there are two new arguments, which tell `splice()` to insert them into the array starting at element 2 (the third one). You may place as many values as you like here to insert as many new elements as you need. The result of making this call is shown in Figure 9-5.

FIGURE 9-5 Inserting values into an array

Advanced Array Splicing

Finally, you can remove and insert elements at the same time, using a call such as the following:

```
Cats.splice(2, 3, 'Siamese', 'Persian')
```

This statement tells `splice()` to use a splice index of 2 (the third element), at which location it must remove three elements and then insert the new values supplied. The result of issuing this call is shown in Figure 9-6.

FIGURE 9-6   Removing from and inserting items into an array

Example files are available in the companion archive demonstrating all three types of splicing. They are *splice.htm*, *insert_splice.htm*, and *advanced_splice.htm*.

Summary

You now know how to use all types of JavaScript arrays, whether single- or multidimensional, numeric, string, associative, or otherwise. Coupled with your earlier knowledge of variables and operators, you are now ready to really get down to some power programming, beginning with Lesson 10 on controlling program flow.

Self-Test Questions

Using these questions, test how much you have learned in this lesson. If you don't know an answer, go back and reread the relevant section until your knowledge is complete. You can find the answers in Appendix A.

1. How can you sort an array alphabetically in ascending order?

2. How can you sort an array alphabetically in descending order?

3. How can you sort an array numerically in ascending order using an external function?

4. How can you sort an array numerically in descending order using an external function?

5. How can you sort an array numerically in ascending order using an inline anonymous function?

6. How can you sort an array numerically in descending order using an inline anonymous function?

7. With which function can you insert and remove elements from an array in the same command?

8. What does the command `fruits.splice(4, 2)` do?

9. What does the command `fruits.splice(5, 0, 'Apples', 'Pears')` do?

10. What does the command `fruits.splice(6, 2, 'Apples', 'Pears', 'Grapes')` do?

Controlling Program Flow

 To view the accompanying video for this lesson, please visit mhprofessional.com/ nixonjavascript/.

Having reached this point in the book, you've actually already learned the vast majority of JavaScript. You should understand how to incorporate it into a web page; the syntax to use; handling numeric variables, strings, and arrays; using operators in expressions according to their associativity; and you've even learned the basics of handling program flow control using the `if()` and `else` keywords.

In this lesson you consolidate your knowledge of the latter so that you can precisely control the flow of program execution.

The `if()` Statement

You've already seen this statement in use a few times, but only with single-line statements, so here's the full syntax of an `if()` statement:

```
if (expression)
{
  // Execute this code, which can be one...
  // ...or more lines
}
```

In this example expression can be any expression at all created using numbers, strings, variables, objects, and operators. The result of the expression must be a Boolean value that can be either `true` or `false`, such as `if (MyVar > 7)`, and so on.

The curly braces encapsulate the code that must be executed upon the expression evaluating to `true`, and there can be none, one, or many statements.

Omitting the Braces

To enable you to create short and simple `if()` statements without having to use braces, they can be omitted if only one statement is to be executed upon the expression being `true`, like this:

```
if (Time < 12) document.write('Good morning')
```

If the code to execute is quite long (so that it might wrap to the following line), you may wish to start it on the following line, but if you do so, because no curly braces are being used to encapsulate the statement, it's best to indent the statement by a few spaces or a tab, so that it clearly belongs to the `if()` statement, like this:

```
if (Time < 12)
  document.write('Good morning. How are you today?')
```

Indeed, if you have a really long statement to execute, it can also be a good idea to split it over several lines at suitable points, like this:

```
if (Time < 12)
  document.write('Good morning. Following is the ' +
    'list of all your appointments for today. The ' +
    'important ones are highlighted in bold')
```

Here I have split the output into three parts by breaking it into three strings, which are displayed one after the other using + operators. I also further indented the follow-on lines to clearly indicate that they belong to the `document.write()` call.

However, in my view this has become a borderline case where you might be better advised to encapsulate the statement within curly braces, because they will ensure there is no ambiguity, and you won't have to worry about the wrapping of long lines diminishing the code readability, like this:

```
if (Time < 12)
{
  document.write('Good morning. Following is the list of all your
appointments for today. The important ones are highlighted in bold')
}
```

Some program editors will automatically indent wrapped-around lines for you (based on the indent at the start of the line), making the code even more readable, and looking like this:

```
if (Time < 12)
{
  document.write('Good morning. Following is the list of
  all your appointments for today. The important ones are
  highlighted in bold')
}
```

In this latter case, the program editor will treat all three lines of the statement as a single line, which they are. Don't try to format your code like this using newlines, though, as it will split it into multiple lines and cause errors—unless you also break the statement into parts, as detailed earlier.

Positioning of Braces

The reason you can lay out your code in a variety of ways is that JavaScript supports the use of tabs, spaces, and newlines as *whitespace*, which is ignored (other than newlines placed within a statement, which indicate a statement end and can be avoided only by splitting statements into parts).

Because of this, programmers can choose to place the curly braces wherever they like. As you have seen, when I use them, I generally place the opening and closing brace directly under the `if()` statement's first character and then indent the encapsulated statements, like this:

```
if (expression)
{
  // Execute this code, which can be one...
  // ...or more lines
}
```

Other programmers, however, choose to place the opening curly brace immediately after the `if()`, like this:

```
if (expression) {
  // Execute this code, which can be one...
  // ...or more lines
}
```

Both of these (and other) types of layout (such as placing the closing curly brace at the end of the final statement) are perfectly acceptable.

There are also some less-used layouts used by other programmers, but the preceding tend to be the main two. I advocate the first type because (even though it requires an extra line of code for each opening brace) it makes the opening braces indent to the level of the closing ones, so that if you have several nested statements, you can more clearly determine that you have the right number of opening and closing braces and that they are all in the right places. It also places more vertical whitespace between the expression and the statements that follow, which I find helpful. However, which system you use is entirely up to you.

The `else` Statement

To accompany the `if()` statement, there's also an `else` keyword, which follows the same rules as `if()`, except the code following an `else` is executed only if the expression following the `if()` evaluates to `false`.

If the code comprises a single statement, it doesn't require encapsulating in curly braces, but if it has two or more statements, braces are required. You use the `else` keyword in conjunction with `if()`, like this:

```
if (Age < 18)
{
  document.write('You are not an adult.')
}
else
{
  document.write('You are an adult.')
}
```

Because both of these keywords only include a single statement, you can safely omit the braces if you wish, like this:

```
if (Age < 18)
  document.write('You are not an adult.')
else
  document.write('You are an adult.')
```

Or, if there's room, you can even move the statements up to directly follow the keywords, like this:

```
if (Age < 18) document.write('You are not an adult.')
else          document.write('You are an adult.')
```

> **Note** In this instance I opted to indent the second statement until it lined up underneath the first one. This helps make it clear what's going on at a glance if I were to come back to this code some months later. However, how you lay out your whitespace is entirely up to you.

There is another convention regarding braces that I recommend you consider using, which is that if one of the statements in an `if()` ... `else` construct uses braces, then so should the other, even if the other one only has a single statement. You can see the difference in the following (all valid) examples, in which I think you'll find that Example 3 (with both sets of statements in braces) is the easiest to follow:

```
if (Age < 18) // Example 1
{
  document.write('You are not an adult.')
  document.write('Sorry, you cannot vote yet.')
}
else
  document.write('You are an adult.')
```

```
if (Age < 18) // Example 2
  document.write('You are not an adult.')
else
{
  document.write('You are an adult.')
  document.write('You can vote.')
}

if (Age < 18) // Example 3
{
  document.write('You are not an adult.')
  document.write('Sorry, you cannot vote yet.')
}
else
{
  document.write('You are an adult.')
}
```

You don't *have* to follow this advice, but it will certainly make your debugging a lot easier if you do, and any other programmers who have to maintain your code will thank you for it.

The `else if()` statement

You can extend the power of `if()` ... `else` even further by also incorporating `else if()` statements, which provide a third option to the original `if()` statement, and which you place before the final `else` statement (if there is one). The following example illustrates how you might use this keyword:

```
if      (Value < 0) document.write('Negative')
else if (Value > 0) document.write('Positive')
else                document.write('Zero')
```

 As with other examples, I have used whitespace liberally in the preceding code to line the statements up and make them easier to follow.

The `else if()` statement follows the same rules as the `if()` and `else` statements with regard to using curly braces to encapsulate multiple statements (but not requiring them for single statements). However, I give the same recommendation as I did earlier that if even one of the parts of an `if()` ... `else if()` ... `else` structure uses braces, then I advise you to use braces for all parts.

Of course, you don't have to use a concluding `else` after an `if()` ... `else if()` construct if you don't want it. For example, if you don't need to deal with the case of a zero value (perhaps because one is not possible in the code you have written), you might simply use the following:

```
if       (Value < 0) document.write('Negative')
else if  (Value > 0) document.write('Positive')
```

Note The purpose of the `else` keyword is as a catch-all, to trap all possible values that remain and execute the statement(s) attached to it if none of the preceding statements in the clause are `true`.

The `switch()` Statement

The `if()`, `else if()`, and `else` statements are very powerful and comprise much of JavaScript programming. But they are not the most efficient method of controlling program flow when there are more than three options to consider. For example, imagine there's an input field on the web page with the following string values from which the user must select their age range:

- 0–1
- 2–3
- 4–6
- 7–12
- 13–17
- 18+

Now here's some code you might use to process the value returned by the input, as shown in Figure 10-1, in which a value of `13-17` has been preselected for the string variable Age (using the *if_else.htm* file from the companion archive):

```
if (Age == '0-1')
{
  document.write('You are a baby.')
  document.write('How can you read this?')
}
```

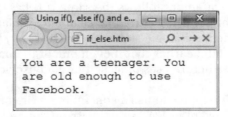

FIGURE 10-1   Using multiple `else if()` statements

```
else if (Age == '2-3')
{
  document.write('You are a toddler.')
}
else if (Age == '4-6')
{
  document.write('You are an infant.')
  document.write('You go to nursery or school.')
}
else if (Age == '7-12')
{
  document.write('You are a child.')
}
else if (Age == '13-17')
{
  document.write('You are a teenager.')
  document.write('You can use Facebook.')
}
else document.write('You are an adult.')
```

Don't you think all those repeated else if() statements are rather cumbersome, and the code feels somewhat heavier than it could be?

Well, the answer is to restructure code such as this using a switch() statement in conjunction with the case and break keywords, like this (as shown in Figure 10-2, created using the *switch.htm* file from the companion archive, and in which the string Age is preassigned the value 4-6):

```
switch(Age)
{
  case '0-1':   document.write('You are a baby.')
                document.write('How can you read this?')
                break
  case '2-3':   document.write('You are a toddler.')
                break
  case '4-6':   document.write('You are an infant.')
                document.write('You go to school now.')
                break
```

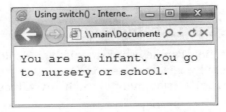

FIGURE 10-2 Using a switch() statement

```
    case '7-12':   document.write('You are a child.')
                   break
    case '13-17':  document.write('You are a teenager.')
                   document.write('You can use Facebook.')
                   break
    default:       document.write('You are an adult.')
}
```

I'm sure you'll agree that using `switch()` statements is a lot clearer than a set of sprawling `else if()`s. To use one, simply place the expression or variable to be tested in the parentheses following the `switch` keyword, then within a pair of curly braces (which are required), provide a number of `case` statements and an optional `default` statement.

Following each `case` keyword, place one possible value that the `switch` variable or expression might have. In this example, `Age` can only have string values, but you can equally test for digits or floating point numbers too. After the possible value, place a colon followed by the statements to execute if the value matches the `switch` variable or expression. In this example, it's one or more `document.write()` statements.

Note how no curly braces are required to contain multiple statements. This is because once the code following the colon starts executing, it will keep on going, executing statement after statement (ignoring the following `case` tests), until `break` or the closing curly brace at the end of the `switch()` statement is encountered.

Using the **break** Keyword

Because program flow will continue to the end of a `switch()` statement (executing all the remaining statements regardless of any following `case` keywords), you must mark the end of a sequence of statements to be executed with a `break` keyword. This causes program flow to jump to just after the closing brace of the `switch()` statement.

You will also encounter the `break` keyword in Lesson 11 where it is used to break to the end of looping structures of code.

Using the **default** Keyword

In the same way that the `else` keyword is a catch-all device for dealing with any other values not caught by `if()` or `else if()` statements, you can use the `default` keyword within a `switch()` statement to catch any values not matched by the `case` statements.

In the previous example, because all possible values for `Age` are tested for except for 18+, then if none of the case statements match, `Age` must contain the value 18+.

Therefore, the default statement is triggered and the statement following it writes the string You are an adult. to the browser.

There is no break keyword after the default option in the preceding example because it is the last statement in the switch() statement, and therefore a break keyword is superfluous in this position, as it would only add extra, unnecessary code. There is, however, nothing stopping you from placing the default statement anywhere within a switch() statement (even at the start), but if you do so, you must add a break keyword after the statements it executes, or program flow will fall through to the following statements, rather than to the end of the switch() statement. However, I recommend that you stick with convention and make default the last clause.

Allowing Fall-Through

Sometimes you may not want to use the break keyword because you wish to allow cases to fall through to other cases. For example, consider the case of wanting to choose the correct language to display on a multinational website. Using a simple input field (or even a geolocation program if you want to be really smart), you could return a string containing the user's country name, for example, perhaps out of the following:

- Australia
- Brazil
- France
- Germany
- Portugal
- Spain
- UK
- USA

Then code to process the country name in the variable Country to a language to use in the variable Language might look like this:

```
switch(Country)
{
  case 'Australia':
  case 'UK':
  case 'USA':
  default:        Language = 'English'
                  break
  case 'Brazil':
  case 'Portugal': Language = 'Portuguese'
                  break
  case 'France':   Language = 'French'
                  break
```

```
case 'Germany':    Language = 'German'
                   break
case 'Spain':      Language = 'Spanish'
}
```

Only after the variable Language has been assigned its value is the break keyword used. Therefore, if any of the countries Australia, UK, or USA are selected, Language is set to English, which is also selected (because the default keyword is included within the fall-through group of cases) for any other value not tested for by the cases in the switch() statement.

A fall-through also occurs for Brazil and Portugal, both of which countries speak Portuguese, but the remaining countries have different languages and don't use any case fall-throughs. Note that there is no break keyword after the final statement, as it is not needed because the end of the switch() has already been reached.

 Yes, I know that many people in the United States speak Spanish, but this is simply an example to explain fall-through. If you wanted to cater for that option, though, you could have two country names for the United States: USA English and USA Spanish, and then simply add a fall-through to the 'Spain' case—while you are at it, you could also add Canada English and Canada French in a similar fashion to cater for its two languages, and so on.

Summary

This lesson concludes everything you need to know to write basic JavaScript programs. You can now handle data in various ways, including variables and arrays; you are able to use complex operators and expressions; and now you can direct the flow of your programs. In the next lesson, therefore, we start to look at more advanced aspects of JavaScript, beginning with putting together various types of looping constructs.

Self-Test Questions

Using these questions, test how much you have learned in this lesson. If you don't know an answer, go back and reread the relevant section until your knowledge is complete. You can find the answers in Appendix A.

1. With which statement can you have JavaScript do something if an expression is true?

2. When are curly braces not required in an if() statement?

3. How can you provide a second option to an if() statement when an expression is false?

4. How can you extend `if()` statements to make further tests?

5. When you wish to test an expression or variable for a range of values and act differently on each, what would be the best statement to use?

6. What keyword is used in `switch()` statements to test a value?

7. What character must follow the value for a case being tested in a `switch()` statement?

8. In a `switch()` statement, which keyword processes all remaining values not specifically handled?

9. In a `switch()` statement, what keyword is used to jump out of the `switch()` to the following statement?

10. Are braces required to enclose the instructions for each case of a `switch()` statement?

Looping Sections of Code

 To view the accompanying video for this lesson, please visit mhprofessional.com/
nixonjavascript/.

In Lesson 10 you learned all about program flow control, branching, and using
if(), else, and switch() statements. These are perfect for altering the
program flow according to values and expressions, but not so good when you need to
repetitively execute a process, such as processing a document a word at a time to find
typographical errors.

This is the type of situation where JavaScript's looping statements come into their
own. With them, you form a loop around a core group of statements and then keep
the loop circulating until (or unless) one or more conditions are met, such as (in the
case of a spelling checker) when the end of the document is reached.

More than that, the different loop types supported also enable you to preassign
values to variables used in the loop, or only enter into a loop if a certain expression is
satisfied.

Using `while()` Loops

The while() statement provides the simplest type of JavaScript loop. In English,
what it does is something like this: "While such-and-such is true, then keep doing
so-and-so until such-and-such is no-longer true, or forever if such-and-such is never
false." Here's an example that displays the 10 times table (shown in Figure 11-1):

```
j = 0

while (j++ < 10)
{
   document.write(j + ' times 10 is ' + j * 10 + '<br>')
}
```

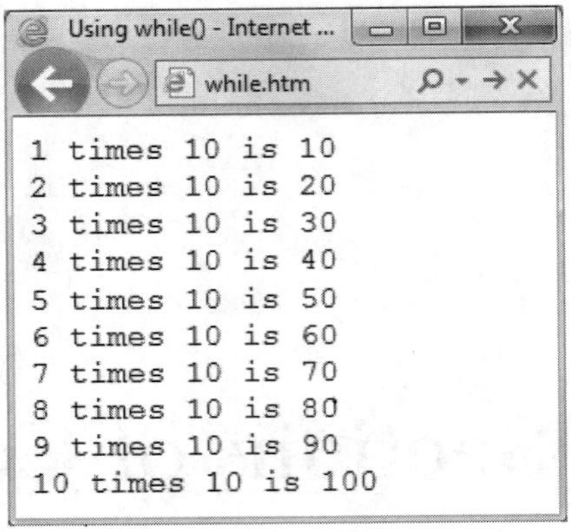

FIGURE 11-1 Using `while()` to calculate the 10 times table

The code used for this and the other examples in this lesson is available in the files *while.htm, do_while.htm, for.htm, for_in.htm, break.htm,* and *continue.htm* in the companion archive.

The Example in Detail

This code starts by initializing the variable j to 0. This variable is used both to decide when to loop (and when to stop looping) and to calculate the times table. Then the `while()` statement tests for j having a value of less than 10. The first time around, its value is 0 so the expression evaluates to `true`. Note also that j is post-incremented after making the test by using the ++ increment operator. This means that the second time around the loop, j will have a value of 1:

```
while (j++ < 10)
```

Inside the braces there is a single statement, which prints the value in j, some text, and then the result of multiplying j by 10. Because j was post-incremented after the test at the start of the loop, it now has a value of 1, so the sentence `'1 times 10 is 10 '` is output to the browser:

```
document.write(j + ' times 10 is ' + j * 10 + '<br>')
```

After the `document.write()` statement is executed, the end of the loop is reached and so program flow returns to the start of the loop once more, where j is once again tested for having a value less than 10.

This time around, it now has a value of 1, so that satisfies the test, and then j is post-incremented, giving it a value of 2. Therefore, this time around the loop, j has a value of 2 and so the sentence 2 `times 10 is 20` is output to the browser, and the loop goes round another time.

This process continues until j has a value of 10, and the test at the start of the loop therefore no longer results in `true`, so program execution jumps to just after the closing brace of the `while()` statement.

Note Because there is only a single statement inside this loop, just as with `for()` statements, you can omit the curly braces if you wish, like this:

```
while (j++ < 10)
    document.write(j + ' times 10 is ' + j * 10 + '<br>')
```

Using do ... while() Loops

With a `while()` loop, if the test at the start is not satisfied, program execution will not flow into the loop. Sometimes, however, you want program flow to go around a loop at least once, in which case it's necessary to perform the loop test afterward.

For example, suppose you wish to calculate the factorial of the number 10 (sometimes displayed mathematically as 10!). This involves multiplying all the numbers from 1 to 10 together, like this: 10 × 9 × 8 × 7 × 6 × 5 × 4 × 3 × 2 × 1.

Using a loop to do this is an efficient method of calculating this value, particularly because once the loop has been built, it can be used to calculate the factorial of any number. And one thing we know for sure about this loop is that it will execute at least once. Therefore, a do ... `while()` structure may be best suited, and you can achieve that like this:

```
j = 10
f = 1

do
{
    f *= j--
} while (j > 0)

document.write('10! is ' + f)
```

One of the neat things about this loop is that f always contains the running total of all previous multiplications, so all that's necessary to do in each iteration is multiply f by the current value in j, save that value back into f, and then decrement j, which is performed by this statement:

```
f *= j--
```

As you will see, the `*=` assignment operator is ideal in this situation, because it performs both the multiplication and the assignment of the result back to f using a single operator. Also, the post-decrement operator applied to j makes for more efficient coding.

The Example in Detail

In detail, what occurs in the preceding example is that j is a loop counter that is initialized, to the value 10 (because there are 10 numbers to multiply) and f is the factorial, which is initialized to 1, as the loop will start with the expression f *= j--, which the first time around the loop will be the equivalent of f = 1 * 10.

The post-decrement operator after the j ensures that each time around the loop the multiplier is decremented by one (but only after the value in j is used in the expression). Therefore, the second time around the loop, f will now have a value of 10, and j will be 9, so the expression will be equivalent to f = 10 * 9.

Then on the next iteration, f will have a value of 90 as it enters the loop and j will be 8, so these two values will be multiplied together and placed back into f. The expressions evaluated in the loop are, therefore, as follows:

```
f =       1 * 10 // Results in 10
f =      10 *  9 // Results in 90
f =      90 *  8 // Results in 720
f =     720 *  7 // Results in 5040
f =    5040 *  6 // Results in 30240
f =   30240 *  5 // Results in 151200
f =  151200 *  4 // Results in 604800
f =  604800 *  3 // Results in 1814400
f = 1814400 *  2 // Results in 3628800
f = 3628800 *  1 // Results in 3628800
```

When the expression at the end of the loop (in the while() part) evaluates to false, this means that j is no longer greater than 0, and so the loop is not reentered, and program flow continues at the first instruction following the loop.

When this example is loaded into a browser (as shown in Figure 11-2), the result shown in the final line is displayed by the document.write() instruction that follows the loop.

 As with many other JavaScript constructs, if there is only one statement inside the loop, you can omit the curly braces if you like, and the loop could therefore be written like this:

```
do f *= j--
while (j > 0)
```

FIGURE 11-2   Using **do ... while()** to calculate the factorial of a number

Using `for()` Loops

Although the preceding two types of loop structures may seem sufficient for most requirements, they can actually be improved on, especially because you must first initialize variables outside of these loops before they are even entered, and then you generally have to increment or decrement at least one variable inside the loop, too.

For these reasons, a third type of loop structure is supported, the `for()` loop, and it is one of the most compact and most used forms of loop structures for these reasons:

- It allows you to initialize all the variables you need within the creation of the loop.
- It allows you to specify the test condition within the creation of the loop.
- It allows you to specify variables to change after each loop iteration within the creation of the loop.

Let's look at how you can do this by rewriting the previous example, as follows:

```
for (j = 10, f = 1 ; j > 0 ; --j)
{
   f *= j
}

document.write('10! is ' + f)
```

Doesn't that look much simpler than the do ... `while()` version? As before, there's still a single statement inside the loop, but it no longer uses the post-decrement operator, because j is decremented within the setup section of the loop. Also, there are no variables preassigned outside of the loop because that is also handled within the loop setup.

The Example in Detail

Here's what's going on. A `for()` loop's setup section (the part within parentheses) is divided into three parts that are separated with semicolons. Each part performs the following, in order:

1. Initializes any variables used within the loop.

2. Performs a test to see whether the loop should be entered.

3. Changes any variables required after each loop iteration.

The first and third sections may include more than one statement as long as you separate them using commas. Therefore, in the first section of the preceding example, j is initialized to a value of 10, and f to a value of 1, like this:

```
j = 10, f = 1
```

Next comes the loop test:

```
j > 0
```

And finally j is decremented:

```
--j
```

With the three sets of arguments inside the brackets looking like this:

```
j = 10, f = 1 ; j > 0 ; --j
```

And that's really all there is to it. When the loop is first entered, the variables are initialized. This will not happen in any other iterations. Then the test in part 2 of the loop setup is made, and if the expression evaluates to true, the loop is entered.

Next, the statements in the loop are executed (in this case there's only one), and then the third section of the loop setup is executed, which in this case decrements j.

Then, the second time and all subsequent times around the loop, section 1 of the setup section is skipped and program flow goes to the third section of the loop setup and then to the test in section 2.

If the test is true, the loop is again entered, the statements in it executed, and then the statements in the third part of the setup section are executed and the loop goes around again if the test still evaluates to true.

But if the test doesn't evaluate to true, program flow goes to the code following the loop, which in this case is the document.write() statement, to print the calculated factorial value.

 Because there is only a single statement within the loop of the preceding example, the braces may legally be omitted from the code, like this (or you can make the code even more compact by placing the statement directly after the loop section):

```
for (j = 10, f = 1; j > 0 ; --j)
    f *= j
```

You can also include additional statements to the third argument of a for() loop by separating them with a comma, like this:

```
for (j = 10, f = 1; j > 0 ; --j, ++f)
```

Generally, for() loops are so powerful that they have become widespread and you will very rarely find that you need to use a while() or do ... while() loop, because for() loops can compactly and neatly accomplish almost every type of looping structure you could want in JavaScript.

Using for (... in ...) Loops

There is another type of for() loop, which was covered in much more detail in Lesson 7. Using the for (... in ...) loop, you can iterate through an array of existing values in an array named Balls, like this:

```
Balls = ['Cricket',
         'Tennis',
         'Baseball',
```

```
        'Hockey',
        'Football']

for (j in Balls)
  document.write(Balls[j] + '<br>')
```

Here, the array `Balls[]` is populated with five string values, and then the `for(... in ...)` loop iterates through them all, assigning an array index (from 0 to that of the index of the final element of the array) to the variable `j`, which is then used within the loop section to print out the value of each element using a `document.write()` statement.

The result of running this code will be as follows:

```
Cricket
Tennis
Baseball
Hockey
Football
```

Breaking Out of a Loop

Amazingly, I haven't yet finished introducing you to everything that JavaScript loops can do for you, because there's still the matter of a couple of keywords you can use to further enhance their use.

The first of these is the `break` keyword, which I already showed being used with `switch()` statements in Lesson 10 to stop fall-through of program flow between cases, but the `break` keyword is not exclusive to `switch()` statements. In fact, it can also be used inside loops.

But why would you want to use a `break` within a loop? Surely, you have all the tests for conditions you could want already? Well, not quite, as it turns out. Sometimes, you may find that something other than the loop counter requires a loop to be exited, and the `break` keyword provides a tidy way to do this.

One reason why you might need to use a `break` keyword is when your loop structure has finished processing and it would be wasteful, pointless, or incorrect for it to continue looping. For example, consider the following code, in which the array `Data` is populated with a set of eight unique items of data (in elements 0 through 7), and the data is being searched to see if the value 11 can be found:

```
Data = [1, 23, 16.3, 88.23, 11, 24.46, 30, 99]

for (j = 0 ; j < Data.length ; ++j)
{
  if (Data[j] == 11) break
}

if (j < Data.length)
    document.write('Found at index ' + j)
else document.write('Not found')
```

A for() loop is being used for the search, and it is simply iterating from element 0 through to the final element index, which can be found by looking up the value of Data.length (length being a property of all arrays, and the period between it and the array name is one means by which JavaScript can access object properties) and subtracting 1 from it. Therefore, as long as the loop variable j is less than that value, the loop will execute.

Within the loop, the if() statement tests for whether the value 11 is found in the current element pointed to by the index loop variable j. If it is, then the value being searched for 11 has been found and there is no reason to search the array any further (because in this instance we know that all the values in the array are unique). Therefore, a break statement is used to break out of the loop and divert program flow to the first statement following it.

In the final two lines, as long as the value in j is still less than Data.length, it represents the index of the array element that contains the value being searched for and displays the fact in the browser, as shown in Figure 11-3 (which illustrates the code searching for two values, the second of which is not in the array); otherwise, the string Not found is displayed.

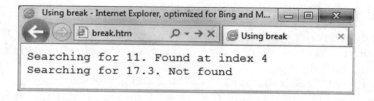

FIGURE 11-3   Using **break** to exit from a loop if a condition is met

As with other JavaScript structures, because this example has only a single statement in the loop, the braces can be omitted for simplicity, like this:

```
for (j = 0 ; j < Data.length ; ++j)
  if (Data[j] == 11) break
```

 When you use the break keyword within a loop that is itself inside one or more other loops, only the current loop will be broken out of because the break keyword applies only to the innermost loop in which it exists.

The continue Statement

The break statement diverts flow to the statement immediately following the loop in which it exists, but sometimes this is too drastic a measure, because you may only want to skip the current iteration of a loop and not all remaining iterations.

When this is the case, you can use the `continue` statement, which forces program flow to skip over any remaining statements in a loop and to start again at the next iteration of the loop. One reason for wanting to do this might be, for example, to avoid encountering a division-by-zero error, which could generate invalid results.

For example, consider the case of some code that must calculate the reciprocal of all numbers between − 5 and 5. The reciprocal of a number is found by dividing the value 1 by that number.

Therefore, if the number happens to be zero, an attempt would be made to divide 1 by 0, which in JavaScript results in the value `Infinity`, which is not a floating point number that can be used in general mathematical expressions, so we need to check for it and remove the possibility, like this:

```
for (j = -5 ; j < 6 ; ++j)
{
  if (j == 0) continue
  document.write('1/' + j + ' is ' + 1 / j + '<br>')
}
```

Figure 11-4 shows this code being run in a browser. As you can see, when the value 0 is reached for j, nothing is displayed, because the `continue` keyword has forced the loop to skip to its next iteration.

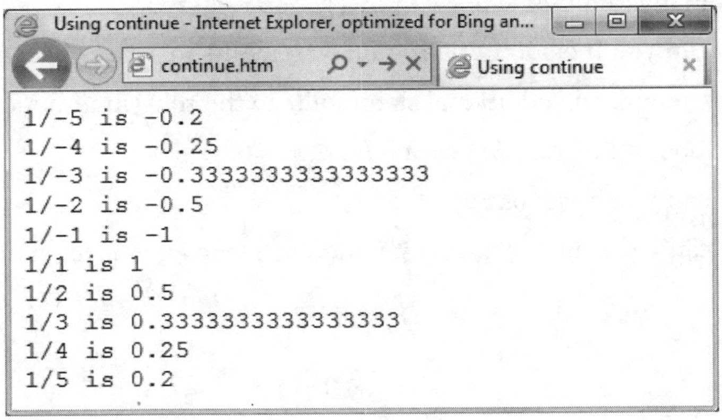

FIGURE 11-4 Using **continue** to skip a loop iteration

Summary

Now that you know how to use the wide variety of looping structures provided by JavaScript, you can begin to develop your own programming style, because it's now possible for you to write most types of code that rely on loops in a number of different ways, and before long, you will begin to settle on the structures that fit your way of thinking the best.

For example, most programmers tend to generally use for() loops, but then they may need to occasionally use the break keyword for special instances, whereas those who prefer while() and do ... while() loops rarely need to use break. It's a matter of personal style. Anyway, whichever types of loop structures you find yourself migrating toward, in Lesson 12 you'll discover even more powerful things you can do with JavaScript, including writing functions and using global and local variables.

Self-Test Questions

Using these questions, test how much you have learned in this lesson. If you don't know an answer, go back and reread the relevant section until your knowledge is complete. You can find the answers in Appendix A.

1. When is the condition of a while() loop tested?

2. When is the condition of a do ... while() loop tested?

3. When is it preferable to use do ... while() in place of while()?

4. Write a simple while() loop to display the 8 times table.

5. How many arguments does a for() loop require?

6. How can you include initialization statements in a for() loop?

7. How can you add additional statements to the third argument of a for() loop?

8. What does a for(... in ...) loop do?

9. How can you break out of a loop?

10. How can you skip the current iteration of a loop and move on to the next iteration?

Writing Functions

To view the accompanying video for this lesson, please visit mhprofessional.com/nixonjavascript/.

Apart from using conditional statements such as if() and switch(), and loops such as while() and for(), there's another way you can control program flow called the *function*. Functions are sections of code that you call from any other part of code (or even the function itself, which is known as *recursion*), and which then perform one or more actions and then return.

When functions return, they may also return a value back to the calling code, or they can simply return without doing so, in which case the returned value will be undefined. Interestingly, as you will learn in Lesson 13, in JavaScript, functions are also objects so they can be passed as values, used in arrays, and so on.

Using Functions

JavaScript comes with many inbuilt functions. For example, to obtain the square root of the number 49, you can call the Math.sqrt() function, like this, which will return the value 7:

```
document.write(Math.sqrt(49))
```

The optional value you pass to a function is called an *argument*, and you can have any number of these arguments, or none. In the case of Math.sqrt(), a single value is required. The square root of that number is then calculated, and the value derived is returned. That's how the document.write() call in the preceding example can display the square root value, because that value is returned directly to the calling code, which is the document.write() call.

There are two types of functions: *named* and *anonymous*. You can create named functions using the keyword function followed by the name to give to the function, and then a pair of parentheses, within which you list the arguments being passed to the function, separated with commas. The code of the function must be enclosed within curly braces.

Following is what the code to emulate the built-in `Math.sqrt()` function might look like, based on the fact that the square root of a number can be calculated by raising that number to the power of 0.5—with `Math.pow()` serving to calculate the power:

```
function SquareRoot(n)
{
   return Math.pow(n, 0.5)
}
```

In this example, the function created is `SquareRoot()`, and it accepts one argument (the value passed in the variable n).

The function code comprises a single statement that simply calls the inbuilt `Math.pow()` function, which accepts two values: a number and a value by which power the number should be raised. So the two values passed to it are n and 0.5.

The `return` Keyword

The function then calculates the square root and returns it, at which point the `return` keyword causes that value to be returned. It is then a simple matter of calling the function in the following manner to display a square root in the browser:

```
document.write(SquareRoot(49))
```

Or, the value returned can be used in an expression, assigned to a variable, or used in numerous other ways.

 Of course, this code slightly cheats because it calls another inbuilt function called `Math.pow()` (in which case we might as well simply call the inbuilt `Math.sqrt()` function in the first place), but it serves to illustrate how to write a simple function that takes one value and returns another after processing it.

Passing Arguments

In the preceding example you saw how to pass a single argument to a function, but you can pass as many as you need (or none), as shown with the following function that provides functionality that is not native to JavaScript (but is in some other languages), namely the ability to create a string by repeating a supplied string a set number of times.

For example, the PHP language provides a function called `str_repeat()`, and the following code gives this same functionality to JavaScript:

```
function StrRepeat(s, r)
{
   return new Array(++r).join(s)
}
```

This function uses the sneaky trick of creating a new array with the number of elements in the value r, plus 1. So if r has the value 3, then the new array is given four elements by pre-incrementing the value in r, resulting in a statement equivalent to new Array(4), as described in Lesson 5.

With the array now created, the join() function is called by attaching it to the Array() function using a period. As you recall from Lesson 7, join() concatenates all the elements in an array into a string, placing the separator string in the value passed to join() between each element value.

Therefore, if r has the value 3, a four-element array is created (with each element being empty). Then the join() function concatenates these four elements together, placing the string in the variable s between each occurrence. Therefore, because the array elements are empty, this entire statement will simply create three copies of the string in s concatenated together, and that is the string that is returned from the function using the return keyword. Neat, huh?

Accessing Arguments

Arguments received by a function are given the names you supply between the parentheses. These do not need to be (and probably will mostly not be) the same names as the variables or values passed to the function.

Variables are assigned to the values received by a function in the order in which they are listed, and there can be as many or as few arguments as you like. Generally, the number of arguments supplied to a function should be the same as the number the function expects to receive, but not always.

If a function receives fewer arguments than it is expecting, it will assign the value undefined to the remaining values, as shown in the following example (see Figure 12-1) in which the third argument has not been passed:

```
Example(1, 2)

function Example(a, b, c)
{
   document.write(a + ' ' + b + ' ' + c)
}
```

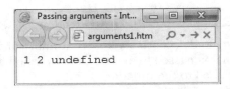

FIGURE 12-1 The third argument has not been passed to the function.

If your function sometimes uses the missing values and sometimes doesn't, this can cause an obscure and hard-to-track down bug. But there are times when you may not want to provide all the arguments to a function, because they may be optional.

For example, consider the inbuilt JavaScript function join() that joins the elements of an array together into a string. It accepts either no argument or an argument that will be used as the divider between each array element. If no argument is supplied, join() assumes a separator string of ', '.

You can write code to perform the same function as join() like this, which creates a function of the same name, but with the first letter of the name capitalized (for simplicity, I have omitted the actual code that does the joining):

```
function Join(separator)
{
  if (separator == undefined) separator = ','
  // do the joining and return the string created
}
```

The key code that provides a default value works like this:

```
if (separator == undefined) separator = ','
```

This can also be achieved using the ternary operator (as described in Lesson 4), thus avoiding the use of an if() statement, like this:

```
separator = !separator ? ',' : separator
```

In this case, the use of the ! symbol before the separator variable stands in for a test for separator having a value of undefined, because the expression returns true if separator is undefined and false if it is defined.

You can also rework this expression to not require the ! symbol and still achieve the same result, like this (which reverses the order of the second and third arguments):

```
separator = separator ? separator : ','
```

If separator is passed as the value 0 or an empty string, the preceding code will not work as intended. Therefore, if you plan to support these two values, you should stick with simply testing whether the separator is defined or not. Incidentally, another way to test a variable (or other object) for not being defined is to use the typeof keyword, for example, if (typeof separator == 'undefined'). With typeof you can also determine whether an object is an array, a string, and so on.

Using the **arguments** Object

Rather than passing and accepting a known number of arguments, you can also access an object that is passed to every function called arguments, which contains every argument passed to the function.

You can access the elements of `arguments` as if it were an array using an index (from 0 to the number of elements in the object minus 1), or iterate through it like this:

```
for (i in arguments)
  document.write(arguments[i])
```

 Though the `arguments` object is not an actual array, it is array-like, and even though you can find its length with `arguments.length` and can access individual elements using an index, you cannot use any array functions on it such as `join()`, because they are set to work only with objects that are of the type `Array`.

Let's look at one example where you might find accessing this object useful by creating a function that accepts any number of arguments and then joins them together into a string, which is returned:

```
function Deobfuscate()
{
  s = ''
  for (e in arguments) s += arguments[e]
  return s
}
```

This is a particularly useful function to have on hand when you wish, for example, to display an e-mail address in a browser, but make it extremely difficult for e-mail harvesting programs to discover, by breaking the e-mail address (or any other section of text) that you wish to obfuscate, like this:

```
document.write(
  Deobfuscate('jame', 'sjone', 's@jjinc', '.com'))
```

This code will make little sense to even the most sophisticated e-mail address harvester, as there are none that I know of that will actually interpret JavaScript to look for e-mail addresses. The result of executing this statement displays in a browser as follows:

jamesjones@jjinc.com

Because `document.write()` can, in some circumstances, overwrite the current document, it is not always the best solution for outputting text. Sometimes, it is better to supply such content to the `innerHTML` property of an object, as this is much safer. For example, you can replace the preceding code with this (*arguments4.htm* in the accompanying archive), which also places the e-mail address in a clickable link:

```
My email address is: <span id='myspan'></span>

<script>
  email = Deobfuscate('jame', 'sjone', 's@jjinc', '.com')
```

```
document.getElementById('myspan').innerHTML =
  "<a href='mailto:" + email + "'>" + email + "</a>"

function Deobfuscate()
{
  s = ''
  for (e in arguments) s += arguments[e]
  return s
}
</script>
```

Using the `this` Keyword

I didn't show you all the code to replicate the `join()` function in the previous section, so let's do that now, using the `this` keyword. Because `join()` can operate on an array without you passing it any argument at all, you may wonder how it knows which array it must work on. The answer is that the array is passed to `join()` using the period operator, like this:

```
Array.join()
```

When the code for the `join()` function begins execution, it obtains the array in the `this` keyword, so we can finish off the new `Join()` function as follows:

```
Array.prototype.Join = Join

function Join(separator)
{
  string    = ''
  separator = typeof separator == 'undefined' ? ',' : separator

  for (j = 0 ; j < this.length -1 ; ++j)
    string += this[j] + separator

  return string + this[j]
}
```

Before the function definition, there is a statement that adds the ability to use the new `Join()` function on `Array` objects. It uses the `prototype` keyword, which is explained in much more detail in Lesson 13 (basically, it allows you to add properties and methods to an object). For now, all you need to know is that the statement allows the function to work.

Inside the function a variable called `string` is initialized to the empty string (`''`). Its value will later be used to return the string created by this function. After that, if `separator` is not defined, it is given the default value of `','`:

```
string    = ''
typeof separator == 'undefined' ? ',' : separator
```

Then a `for()` loop is used to iterate through all elements in the array `this`, except for the last one. You will recall that the `this` keyword contains the argument supplied via the period operator—in this case, an `Array` object:

```
for (j = 0 ; j < this.length -1 ; ++j)
```

Each time around the loop, the value in the current array element is appended to the variable `string`, followed by the separator:

```
string += this[j] + separator
```

Finally, once the loop has completed, there is one element remaining in the array that hasn't yet been accessed, and so that is appended to the end of `string`, and then the value in `string` is returned:

```
return string + this[j]
```

Code such as the following can now be used to access the new function:

```
Pets = ['cats', 'dogs', 'rabbits']
document.write(Pets.Join(' and '))
```

This code creates a three-element array with the names of three types of pets, then it passes that array to the `Join()` function using the period operator and also supplies the string ` and ` to be used as a separator. Figure 12-2 shows the result of loading the code (*this.htm* in the companion archive) into a browser.

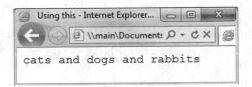

FIGURE 12-2   Using the `this` keyword

 As well as using `this` to pass values using the period operator, in Lesson 13 you'll learn how the `this` keyword is also very useful for attaching functions to JavaScript events.

Anonymous Functions

In JavaScript it is not always necessary to give a name to a function, and functions without names are called *anonymous* functions. One reason for using an anonymous function is when it is called only once by one statement, and so for reasons of logic and code readability, the function is inserted anonymously in the code at the point where it is needed.

For example, as you will learn in Lesson 16, it is easy to attach JavaScript functions to events that occur in the browser. For example, you may want to execute a couple of actions when a mouse passes over an object, and a function is a good way to do this, as follows:

```
MyObject.onmouseover = DoThese

function DoThese()
{
  // Do this
  // DO that
  // Do the other
}
```

But if this function is only to be called at this particular point in the code, you can simplify things by making the function anonymous, like this:

```
MyObject.onmouseover = function()
{
  // Do this
  // DO that
  // Do the other
}
```

Now you are no longer cluttering up the JavaScript name space with the function name DoThese, and the code is shorter and sweeter.

Note If you want to reuse the function code in other places, it then becomes wasteful to use it in anonymous functions, because you will end up with several occurrences of the function's code. Therefore, anonymous functions are optimal only when they will be called by a single statement.

Global and Local Variable Scope

Up to this point I have left out a very important keyword that you will certainly have seen if you have viewed the source of any JavaScript code, and that's the var keyword. After introducing it here, you'll see me using it a lot more. However, I left out its inclusion until now because I didn't want to get you bogged down by the difference between *local* and *global* variables. But you are ready for it now!

So far I have treated all the variables created in the book as having global scope. This means that once defined, you can access their values and modify them from any other part of a program. But often this isn't desirable because you can·start to run out of good variable names and, as a program gets longer, so will your variable names.

More than that, the larger and more complicated a program gets and the more people working on it, the greater the chance that you may inadvertently reassign a value to a variable that is being used in another part of the program, resulting in name clashes and weird values creeping in, creating very difficult-to-trace bugs.

Using Local Variables

The solution to a sprawling name space packed with numerous variable names is to allow functions to reuse a variable name without it affecting the value of any variable with the same name used outside of the function. And the way this is achieved is with the var keyword.

To tell JavaScript that a variable you are using within a function should have local scope only, you simply precede it with the var keyword where it is first assigned a value, like this:

```
var MyVar = 42
```

From then on, this variable will have its value only within the function call (and any subfunctions that might be created within it). When the function returns, the variable's value is forgotten, and if there is a global variable of the same name, it will retain its value because local variables don't affect it.

 There is no point whatsoever in using the var keyword outside of a function, as you often see in examples of code on the Internet, because the program scope at that point is global and so applying local scope in a global environment results only in the variable having global scope. One reason instructors may do this, though, is when they think you may take their sample code and place it within a function. In this case it really is a good idea to make all variables that are used purely within the function have only local scope. Therefore, it can be a good habit for beginners to adopt.

To illustrate how to use the var keyword, let's revisit the Join() function we looked at a little earlier, but this time with var keywords in the right places (shown in bold text):

```
function Join(separator)
{
  var string = ''
  separator = typeof separator == 'undefined' ? ',' : separator

  for (var j = 0 ; j < this.length -1 ; ++j)
    string += this[j] + separator

  return string + this[j]
}
```

As you'll recall, this is the replacement function written to emulate the built-in join() function. But as previously written, it was wasteful on global name space by treating both `string` and `j` as global variables, when there was no valid reason for this, and it could cause a bug if there were any existing global variables of these names.

Instead, because `string` and `j` are meant for use only in passing, the first time each is accessed (even if it's inside the setup part of a `for()` loop, as in this case), it is preceded by a `var` keyword, which ensures it will only have scope within this function.

 Once the `var` keyword has been applied to a variable, it does not need to be done again. The local scope will remain until the function returns.

In the following example, the variable `Fred` is assigned the value 1. Because the assignment occurs outside of any functions, it has global scope, which means its value can be accessed from any part of the program.

However, within the function `MyFunc()` the variable `Fred` is reused, but with the `var` keyword preceding it, so it has local scope only.

```
Fred = 1
document.write('Fred is ' + Fred + '<br>')
MyFunc()
document.write('Fred is ' + Fred + '<br>')

function MyFunc()
{
  var Fred = 2
  document.write('Fred is ' + Fred + '<br>')
}
```

Following the program flow, at the first `document.write()` call Fred has a value of 1. Then `MyFunc()` is called and, within the function, the local variable `Fred` is assigned the value 2. After displaying its value, the function returns (no `return` keyword is used because there is no value to return from this function).

Upon return, the value in `Fred` is again displayed, and it is back to 1 again, because when `Fred` is referred to outside of the function, it refers to the global variable, whose value remains unchanged at 1.

Figure 12-3 (created with *var.htm* in the companion archive) shows the result of running this code in a browser.

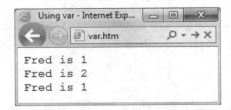

FIGURE 12-3   Using local and global variables of the same name

What is happening here is that two separate variables have been used. They may have the same name, but because the one in the function is given local scope, it is quite different from the one outside the function. I would also like to mention in passing that the keyword `var` is not actually very helpful in that it doesn't really describe what it does. In my view the keyword `local` would have been a much better choice. Nevertheless, `var` is the word that has been chosen—just remember that it always applies local scope (and only works within a function).

Global Naming Convention

I write a lot of JavaScript code and found that for each variable used I would still have to keep referring back to see whether it had a `var` keyword applied at any point in a function (making it local), or if no `var` keyword was used, it would then be global. To save me from having to keep rechecking, I came up with the following simple convention.

Whenever a variable is created that should have global scope, I use all uppercase letters, like this:

```
HIGHSCORE  = 0    // Creates a global variable
HighScore += 100 // Increments a local variable
```

Therefore, I can be sure that any variables I use that have any lowercase letters are being used as local variables, and I also ensure I use the `var` keyword on their first use in a function.

Of course, you can use any other convention you like (such as prefacing global variables with G_), or no convention at all.

 You might ask whether separating global and local variables by uppercase and lowercase obviates the need for the `var` keyword, as local variables will never compete with global ones. However, that's not the case because all variables would then be global and we would be back at having to choose lots of different non-uppercase variable names for use in functions in order to avoid them conflicting with each other. Therefore, using uppercase for global variables simply makes it clear at a glance which ones are and aren't global, so you never have to go hunting for `var` keywords to understand the various scopes of variables in a complex function.

Summary

Congratulations! With the use of functions under your belt, you can now call yourself a JavaScript programmer. However, there are still a few more steps to take before you can call yourself a master of the language—starting in the following lesson with JavaScript objects, which enable you to write OOP (Object-Oriented Programming).

Self-Test Questions

Using these questions, test how much you have learned in this lesson. If you don't know an answer, go back and reread the relevant section until your knowledge is complete. You can find the answers in Appendix A.

1. What is the main purpose of a function?

2. What is an anonymous function?

3. When should you *not* use an anonymous function?

4. What is the main means by which a value is returned by a function?

5. How can values be passed to a function?

6. How does a function access the values passed to it?

7. What is another way of accessing the arguments passed to a function?

8. In what circumstance is it preferable to use the `arguments` object rather than named arguments?

9. How is the `this` object used by a function?

10. How can you tell a function that a variable is to be used only locally?

13

Manipulating JavaScript Objects

 To view the accompanying video for this lesson, please visit mhprofessional.com/ nixonjavascript/.

JavaScript is an interesting language in that everything in it is an object. Arrays are objects, functions are objects, variables are objects, and so on, although they are objects of different types, or should I say *class*.

You see, by being structured this way, JavaScript is extremely easy to enhance by adding new classes (or types) of objects and then creating objects using these classes with the new keyword, as you've seen used for creating new arrays, for example.

You've also seen the prototype keyword used to allow a new function to be created to extend the JavaScript language by, for example, adding new functions to manipulate objects of the type Array. In this chapter I bring all these things (and more) together and show how you can create truly Object-Oriented Programs (OOP).

Declaring a Class

The first step in object-oriented programming is declaring a class, which defines a new type of object but doesn't actually create the object. Classes group together a combination of data and the program code required to manipulate the data into a single object.

To declare a class you use the same syntax as for a function (because functions in JavaScript are actually objects), like this:

```
function UserClass(firstname, lastname)
{
  this.firstname = firstname
  this.lastname  = lastname
```

```
  this.getName = function()
  {
    return this.firstname + ' ' + this.lastname
  }
}
```

This code is known as a class *constructor*. It creates the new class `UserClass` and gives it two items of data it can hold: `firstname` and `lastname`.

It also sets up a method (another name for a function) that can be applied to the class called `getName()`, which returns a string with `firstname` and `lastname` concatenated together, separated with a space character.

 See how the `this` keyword is used here to reference objects created using this class and the functions supplied to access the data in the object. You will also have noticed how an anonymous function is assigned to `this.getName`. This is a good use of an anonymous function, as it's the only place the function is accessed. However, a name does get indirectly assigned to this function after all, because the function can be accessed through calling the `getName()` method on any objects created from the class.

Creating an Object

You can now create a new object (known as an *instance*) based on this class, as follows (in which the new object `User` is created):

```
User = new UserClass()
```

This creates the new object `User`, which has all the properties and methods defined in the class. The object doesn't (yet) have any data in it, though.

By the way, in JavaScript, the terms *method* and *function* mean the same thing and are interchangeable. However, I choose to refer to a function by the name method only when it is provided as part of a class declaration, and is therefore a method that can be used on objects that are instances of the class. And I reserve the term function for stand-alone functions that are not part of OOP.

Accessing Objects

Once an instance of a class has been created using the new keyword, you can populate the object with data like this:

```
User.firstname = 'Julie'
User.lastname  = 'Smith'
```

Or, alternatively, you can pre-populate the object (in the same manner as pre-populating a new array) when you create the instance of the class, like this:

```
User = new UserClass('Julie', 'Smith')
```

Thereafter, you can read these properties back by accessing them in the following manner:

```
document.write(User.firstname)
```

And you can update object properties (in the case of this instance, for example) with a change of the user's last name, like this:

```
User.lastname = 'Jones'
```

And you can call any of the methods provided by an object's class, such as the getName() method of the UserClass class, like this:

```
document.write(User.getName())
```

Figure 13-1 shows the result of running the preceding code (available as *class.htm* in the companion archive) in a browser.

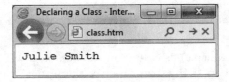

FIGURE 13-1 Calling the getName() method on the User object

The **prototype** Keyword

The prototype keyword can save you a lot of memory. For example, in the UserClass class, every instance will contain the two properties and the method. Therefore, if you have a thousand of these objects in memory, the method getName() will also be replicated a thousand times—this is highly wasteful.

However, because the method is identical in every case, you can specify that new objects should refer to a single instance of the method only instead of creating a copy of it. To do this, instead of using the following in a class constructor:

```
this.getName = function()
```

You can replace the statement with this:

```
UserClass.prototype.getName = function()
```

What is happening here is that instead of attaching the function to the this keyword (which would cause multiple instances of the function), the function is attached directly to the class UserClass via the prototype keyword.

All methods have a prototype property designed to hold properties and methods that are not to be replicated in objects created from the class. Instead, when the prototype keyword is used, the method (or property) is passed by *reference* so that there will only be one instance of the method (or property).

This passing by reference means you can add a prototype property or method to a class at any time and all objects (even those already created) will inherit it. For example, if you wish to create a standard message that will be used to create users logging into a website, you could extend the UserClass class with the following:

```
UserClass.prototype.Greeting = 'Welcome back '
```

This type of method or property (created using the prototype keyword) is known as *static*. A static method or property has a single instance that is accessible from any object created from a class.

You can display this single instance of the property at any time from any object created from the class, like this:

```
document.write(User.Greeting)
```

You could then expand the getName() method to supply the greeting, like this:

```
UserClass.prototype.getName = function()
{
   return this.Greeting + this.firstname + ' ' + this.lastname
}
```

Now, when getName() is called on the object, it will display the following (pulling the Greeting string from the prototype of the class so that only a single instance of the string exists, no matter how many instances of the object there are):

Welcome back Julie Smith

Extending JavaScript Functions

In Lesson 12 I briefly glossed over the prototype keyword when showing you how to attach a new function (now called a method, because we're discussing OOP) to objects of the type Array. Now that you have read this far, you should understand exactly what was going on.

In the replacement Join() method, the Array class has its prototype property updated by adding to it a new method called Join().

I have updated the example, shown next, by assigning the method directly to Array.prototype.Join (rather than first creating the method, giving it a name, and then assigning that name to Array.prototype.Join, as was previously the case):

```
Array.prototype.Join = function(separator)
{
   var string = ''
   separator  = typeof separator == 'undefined' ? ',' : separator

   for (var j = 0 ; j < this.length -1 ; ++j)
      string += this[j] + separator

   return string + this[j]
}
```

You should now see how this code simply adds a new static method to the `Array` class so that it can be called on any object of that type, like this:

```
MyArray.Join()
```

You can extend any of JavaScript's classes in a similar manner, even to the point of rewriting it to work the way you prefer, as is the case with frameworks such as *jQuery* (see *jquery.com*), which extensively extends JavaScript to provide a wide range of additional functionality.

For example, if you wanted to make the `StrRepeat()` function from Lesson 12 operate as a method on `String` objects, you could use the following code to add a method called `Repeat()`:

```
String.prototype.Repeat = function(r)
{
   return new Array(++r).join(this)
}
```

Then, for example, to display the string `'Hip, Hip, Hooray. '` three times, you can use the following statement (shown in Figure 13-2):

```
document.write('Hip, Hip, Hooray. '.Repeat(3))
```

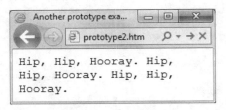

FIGURE 13-2 Implementing a new `Repeat()` method

 In the preceding example, rather than attaching to a string variable, the `repeat()` method is attached directly to a string. To JavaScript, this is the same thing because such a string is an object of type `String`.

Summary

You are now becoming a power JavaScript programmer, capable of bending the will of the language itself to your desire. All that remains to finish your training (before moving on to using JavaScript in meaningful ways in your web pages) is to enhance your knowledge a bit by looking at things such as how to gracefully handle errors in your code and how to use regular expressions for powerful pattern matching—both of which are in the following lesson.

Self-Test Questions

Using these questions, test how much you have learned in this lesson. If you don't know an answer, go back and reread the relevant section until your knowledge is complete. You can find the answers in Appendix A.

1. What syntax do you use to declare a class?

2. How do you create a new instance of a class?

3. In a class declaration, how do you declare properties?

4. In a class declaration, how do you declare methods?

5. How can you access a property of an object created from a class?

6. How can you access a method of an object created from a class?

7. What is the purpose of the `prototype` keyword?

8. What is a static property or method?

9. How do you apply the `prototype` keyword?

10. How can you extend JavaScript by adding new functions?

Handling Errors and Regular Expressions

 To view the accompanying video for this lesson, please visit mhprofessional.com/nixonjavascript/.

There's no getting away from it, even the most careful programmers build unexpected errors (or bugs) into their code, and so will you—it's perfectly normal. And even after you think you've fully debugged your code, the likelihood remains that there may still be obscure bugs lurking somewhere.

The last thing you want on a published website is for users to encounter errors, or sometimes even worse, just find your code doesn't work for them—making them leave to never return. But JavaScript comes with ways you can minimize the problem by placing helper code around statements where you suspect a bug may be that will take over if one occurs.

In this lesson I show you how you can use JavaScript's in-built error trapping for dealing with bugs, and even for managing cross-browser compatibility. I also show you how you can use regular expressions to perform powerful and complex pattern matching in single statements.

Using onerror

The simplest way to catch errors in your code is to attach a new function to the onerror event, like this:

```
window.onerror = function(msg, url, line)
{
  var temp = url.split('/')
```

```
url       = temp[temp.length - 1]

alert('Error in line ' + line + ' of ' + url + '\n\n' + msg)
}
```

The `onerror` event passes three values to a function attached to it: an error message, the URL of the page where the error was encountered, and the line number of the error. The new function in the preceding example accepts these values in the variables `msg`, `url`, and `line`.

The function code then calls the in-built JavaScript `split()` function, which splits a string (in this case `url`) at whatever character is supplied to it (in this case `'/'`) into an array of elements containing each of the parts split out from the string, like this:

```
var temp = url.split('/')
```

Then the final element (indexed by `temp.length - 1`) is placed back into the variable `url`, like this:

```
url = temp[temp.length - 1]
```

The result of these two lines of code is to strip any path details from `url`, leaving only the name of the file in which the error occurred. If this is not done, on deeply nested pages a very large string would be displayed, making the error message very hard to read.

Having shortened `url`, the in-built JavaScript `alert()` function is called, passing it the details to display, like this:

```
alert('Error in line ' + line + ' of ' + url + '\n\n' + msg)
```

Therefore, for example, with this function in place, if you then introduce a mistake into your code such as the following example (in which the final e is omitted from `document.write`), the result will be similar to Figure 14-1:

```
document.writ('Test')
```

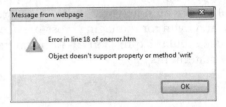

FIGURE 14-1 Attaching an alert window to the `onerror` event

 Rather than using `<br>` tags to obtain the newlines in the alert dialog (which will not work because dialog boxes don't support HTML), I have used the string `\n\n`, which translates into two newline characters.

Using this function, you can quickly and easily catch the bulk of bugs in your code before transferring it to a production server. I don't recommend leaving this function in place on customer-facing websites, though.

It would probably be better to write a more obscure message along the lines of "Sorry, this web page encountered an error, please try again." Hopefully whatever caused the error will not be in place on the second attempt, as you will have thoroughly debugged most non-obscure bugs already.

Limiting the Scope of `onerror`

Apart from attaching to the `window` object to trap all errors that may arise in a given window, you can attach to other objects too. For example, if it is so critical that a particular image should load that you need to do something if it doesn't, you could use code such as this:

```
<img src='image.jpg' onerror='fixError()'>
```

Now write whatever code you need to correct for the missing image and place it in a function called `fixError()` in order to deal with the error event if it occurs. Likewise, if you wish to trap errors only in a section of a document (and not the whole window), you can place that part in an element such as a `<div>` and attach the `onerror` event to it like this:

```
<div onerror='fixError()'>
  // Contents of div
</div>
```

Using `try` ... `catch()`

Rather than just catching errors and displaying debugging information, you can go a step further and choose to ignore errors that may be trivial.

For example, if you have some code that you know works only in some browsers but causes errors in others, it would be a shame to not allow the added functionality to at least some of your users. And you can do this by placing such code in a `try` ... `catch()` structure.

The way you do this is as follows, in which the code to try and code to call upon the first code causing an error are placed in the two parts of the structure:

```
try
{
  // Place code to try here.
}
catch(e)
{
  // Place alternate code here.
}
```

The argument passed to the `catch()` part of the structure is an error object, which can be used for obtaining the error message by displaying its `message` property, like this (as shown in Figure 14-2 in which an attempt to access the object `MyObject` has failed because it doesn't exist):

```
catch(e)
{
   alert('Error: ' + e.message)
}
```

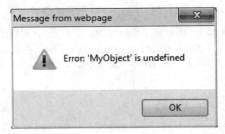

FIGURE 14-2 Using `try` and `catch()`

The code used for creating Figure 14-2 is in the *try_catch.htm* file in the accompanying archive.

Ignoring the Error

If you wish, you can ignore the error object and simply get on with executing alternative code. For example, you will see the following code used in Lesson 20 for creating an object with which Ajax (Asynchronous JavaScript And XML) background communication can be initiated with a web server:

```
try
{
   var ajax = new XMLHttpRequest()
}
catch(e1)
{
   try
   {
     ajax = new ActiveXObject("Msxml2.XMLHTTP")
   }
   catch(e2)
   {
     try
     {
       ajax = new ActiveXObject("Microsoft.XMLHTTP")
     }
```

```
    catch(e3)
    {
      ajax = false
    }
  }
}
```

For reasons that are explained in Lesson 20, it can take up to three attempts to create an Ajax object, depending on the browser used, and the preceding code handles all this gracefully to return an Ajax object in `ajax`, if the browser supports it.

Regular Expressions

Regular expressions were invented as a means of matching an enormous variety of different types of patterns with just a single expression. Using them, you can replace several lines of code with a simple expression and can even use regular expressions in replace as well as search operations.

To properly learn everything there is to know about regular expressions could take a whole book (and, indeed, books have been written on the subject), so I'm just going to introduce you to the basics in this lesson, but if you need to know more, I recommend you check out the following URL as a good starting point: *wikipedia.org/wiki/Regular_expression*.

In JavaScript you will use regular expressions mostly in two functions: `test()` and `replace()`. The `test()` function tells you whether its argument matches the regular expression, whereas `replace()` takes a second parameter: the string to replace the text that matches.

Using `test()`

Let's say you want to find out whether one string occurs within another. For example, if you wish to know whether the string `whether` occurs in Hamlet's famous soliloquy, you might use code such as the following:

```
s = "To be, or not to be, that is the question: "   +
    "Whether 'tis Nobler in the mind to suffer "     +
    "The Slings and Arrows of outrageous Fortune, "  +
    "Or to take Arms against a Sea of troubles, "    +
    "And by opposing end them."

RegExp = /whether/
document.write(RegExp.test(s))
```

The `test()` function requires passing the regular expression to it via the period operator, and the string to be searched must be passed as an argument between the parentheses.

In this example, the object RegExp is a regular expression object that is given the value /whether/, which is how you denote a regular expression. First, you place a / character, then the text to match, followed by a closing / character.

In this example, however, a match is not made because (by default) regular expressions are case sensitive, and only the word Whether (with an uppercase W) exists in the string.

If you wish to make a case-insensitive search, you can tell JavaScript this by placing the letter i after the closing / character, like this (in this case, a match will be made):

```
RegExp = /whether/i
```

You don't have to place a regular expression in an object first if you choose not to, so the two lines can be replaced with the following single statement:

```
document.write(/whether/i.test(s))
```

Using `replace()`

You can also replace text that matches using the replace() function. The source string is not modified by this because replace() returns a new string with all the changes made.

Therefore, for example, to replace the string 'tis in the soliloquy with the word it's (although Shakespeare would surely object), you could use a regular expression and the replace() function like this:

```
document.write(s.replace(/'tis/, "it's"))
```

 Note The replace() function takes its arguments differently than test(). First, it requires that the string for matching against is passed to it via the period operator. Then it takes two arguments in parentheses: the regular expression and the string to replace any matches with.

Figure 14-3 shows the result of executing this statement (using the file *replace.htm* in the accompanying archive). In it you can see that the word after Whether is now it's.

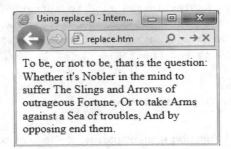

FIGURE 14-3   Applying `replace()` to a string

As with `test()` you can specify a case-insensitive replace by placing an `i` character at the end of the regular expression, as in the following example, which replaces the first occurrence of the word `to` in any combination of uppercase and lowercase, with the word `TO` in uppercase:

```
document.write(s.replace(/to/i, "TO"))
```

Replacing Globally

You can also choose to conduct a global replacement and replace all occurrences of a match by placing the character `g` after the expression, as follows:

```
document.write(s.replace(/to/ig, "TO"))
```

In the preceding example both the characters `i` and `g` have been placed after the expression, so this causes a global, case-insensitive search-and-replace operation, resulting in Figure 14-4 in which you can see all incidences of the word `to` have been changed to uppercase.

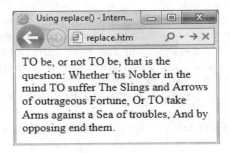

FIGURE 14-4   Performing a global, case-insensitive replace operation

Fuzzy Matching

Regular expressions are a lot more powerful than simply searching for and replacing words and phrases, because they also support complex fuzzy logic features through the use of *metacharacters*.

There are several types of metacharacters, but let's look at just one for now, the `*` character, to see how they work. When you place a `*` in a regular expression, it is not treated as that asterisk character, but as a metacharacter with a special meaning, which is that when performing a match, the character immediately preceding the `*` may appear in the searched string any number of times (or not at all).

This type of metacharacter is particularly useful for sweeping up lots of blank space so that you can, for example, search for any of the strings `'back pack'`, `'backpack'`, `'back  pack'` (with two spaces between the words), `'BackPack'` (with mixed case), and many other combinations, like this:

```
s = "Have you seen my BackPack anywhere?"

document.write(/back *pack/i.test(s))
```

Because the i character is also used, the matching is case insensitive, and so the word BackPack is found by the regular expression, and the document.write() call displays the result of true in the browser.

 If you want to use any of the characters that are metacharacters as regular characters in your regular expressions, you must escape them by preceding the characters with a \ character. For example, * will turn the * from a metacharacter into a simple asterisk.

Matching Any Character

You can get even fuzzier than that, though, with the period (or dot) character, which can stand in for any character at all (except a newline). For example, to find all HTML tags (which start with < and end with >), you could use the following regular expression (in either a test() or replace() call):

```
/<.*>/
```

The left- and right-angle brackets on the sides serve as the start and end points for each match, respectively. Within them this expression will match any character due to the dot metacharacter, while the * after the dot says there can be zero, one, or any number of these characters. Therefore, any size of HTML tag, from the meaningless <> upward, will be matched.

Other metacharacters include the + symbol, which works like *, except that it will match one or more characters, so you could avoid matching <> by ensuring there is always at least one character between the angle brackets, like this:

```
/<.+>/
```

Unfortunately, because the * and + characters will match all the way up to the last > on a line, the previous expression will catch entire elements with start and end tags like <h1>A Heading</h1>, as well as nested HTML such as <h1>A Heading</h1>. We need a way to stop at the first > character.

Not Matching a Character

A solution to the multi-tag matching problem is to use the ^ character whose meaning is "anything but," but which must be placed within square brackets, like this:

```
[^>]+
```

This regular expression is like .+ except that there is one character it refuses to match, the > character. Therefore, when presented with the string <h1>A Heading</h1>, the expression will now stop at the first > encountered, and so the initial <h1> tag will be properly matched. Table 14-1 summarizes the basic metacharacters and their actions.

TABLE 14-1   The Basic Metacharacters

Metacharacters	Action
/	Begins and ends a regular expression
.	Matches any character other than newline
*	Matches previous element zero or more times
+	Matches previous element one or more times
?	Matches previous element zero or one time
[characters]	Matches a single character out of those contained within the brackets
[^characters]	Matches a single character that is not contained within the brackets
(regexp)	Treats *regexp* as a group for counting, or following *, + or ?
left|right	Matches either *left* or *right*
l-r	(Within square brackets) Matches a range of characters between *l* and *r*
^	(Outside of square brackets) Requires the match to be at the search string's start
$	(Outside of square brackets) Requires the match to be at the search string's end

I have already explained some of the characters in Table 14-1, whereas some should be self-explanatory. Others, however, you may find confusing, so I would recommend only using those you understand until you have learned more about regular expressions, perhaps from the Wikipedia article listed a little earlier.

There is also a selection of escape metacharacters and numeric ranges you can include, listed in Table 14-2.

To help you better understand how these various metacharacters can work together, in Table 14-3 I have detailed a selection of regular expression examples and the matches they will make.

Remember that you can place the character i after the closing / of a regular expression to make it case insensitive, and place a g to perform a global search (or replace).

You can also place the character m after the final / which puts the expression into multiline mode, so that the ^ and $ characters will match at the start and end of any newlines in the string, respectively, rather than the default of the string's start and end.

Note   You may use any combination of the i, g, and m modifiers after your regular expressions.

TABLE 14-2 Escape and Numeric Range Metacharacters

Other	Action
\b	Matches a word boundary
\B	Matches where there isn't a word boundary
\d	Matches a digit (equivalent to [0–9])
\D	Matches a non-digit (equivalent to [^0–9])
\n	Matches a newline character
\s	Matches a whitespace character (any of the following: space, tab, carriage return, newline, or form feed)
\S	Matches a non-whitespace character
\t	Matches a tab character
\w	Matches one of a–z, A–Z, 0–9, or _
\W	Matches any character except a–z, A–Z, 0–9, or _
\x	(Where x is a metacharacter) Treats x as a normal character
{n}	Matches exactly n times
{n,}	Matches n times or more
{min,max}	Matches at least *min* and at most *max* times

TABLE 14-3 Some Example Regular Expressions and Their Matches *(Continued)*

Example	Matches
\.	The first . in "Hello there. Nice to see you."
h	The first h in "My hovercraft is full of eels"
lemon	The word lemon in "I like oranges and lemons"
orange|lemon	Either orange or lemon in "I like oranges and lemons"
bel[ei][ei]ve	Either believe or beleive (also beleeve or beliive)
bel[ei]{2}ve	Either believe or beleive (also beleeve or beliive)
bel(ei)|(ie)ve	Either believe or beleive (but not beleeve or beliive)
2\.0*	2., 2.0, 2.00, and so on
j-m	Any of the characters j, k, l, or m
house$	Only the final house in "This house is my house"
^can	Only the first can in "can you open this can?"

TABLE 14-3   Some Example Regular Expressions and Their Matches

Example	Matches
\d{1,2}	Any one- or two-digit number from 0 to 9 and 00 to 99
[\w]+	Any group of at least one-word character
[\w]{3}	Any group of three-word characters

Summary

This lesson has covered some fairly advanced things, including error handling and sophisticated pattern matching, and it tops off the last items of basic knowledge you need for the JavaScript language. Starting with the following lesson I will, therefore, concentrate on how to use JavaScript to interact with web pages, commencing with understanding how JavaScript integrates with the Document Object Model (DOM) of HTML to create dynamic functionality.

Self-Test Questions

Using these questions, test how much you have learned in this lesson. If you don't know an answer, go back and reread the relevant section until your knowledge is complete. You can find the answers in Appendix A.

1. With which event can you trap JavaScript errors?

2. How can you trap errors (a) in a whole document and (b) only in part of a document?

3. With which statement can you mark a section of code to be tried by a browser but not issue an error if it fails?

4. How can you deal with an error that has been encountered in the manner of question 3?

5. What is a regular expression?

6. Which character is used to denote both the start and end of a regular expression?

7. With which functions can you (a) check a string using a regular expression and (b) modify a string with a regular expression?

8. In a regular expression, which metacharacter represents whitespace?

9. In a regular expression, what is a shorter way to express this set of characters: abcdefghijk?

10. Which two characters can you place after a regular expression to ensure the expression is applied both case insensitively and globally?

Interacting with the Document Object Model

 To view the accompanying video for this lesson, please visit mhprofessional.com/ nixonjavascript/.

The Document Object Model (DOM) separates the different parts of an HTML document into a hierarchy of objects, each one having its own *properties*. The term *property* is used for referring to an attribute of an object such as the HTML it contains, its width and height, and so on.

The outermost object possible is the window object, which is the current browser window, tab, iframe, or popped-up window. Underneath this is the document object, of which there can be more than one (such as several documents loaded into different iframes within a page). And inside a document there are other objects such as the head and body of a page.

Within the head there can be other objects such as the title and meta objects, while the body object can contain numerous other objects, including headings, anchors, forms, and so forth.

The DOM

Figure 15-1 shows a representation of the DOM of an example document, with the document title of *Example*, a meta tag in the head, and three HTML elements (a link, a form, and an image) in the body section.

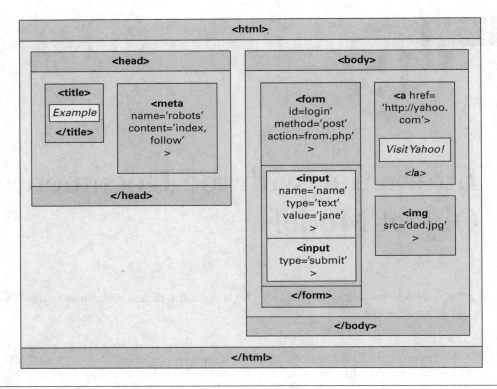

FIGURE 15-1 Example of a DOM showing head and body sections

The source of this example web page looks like this:

```
<!DOCTYPE html>
<html>
  <head>
    <title>Example</title>
    <meta name='robots' content='index, follow'>
  </head>
  <body>
    <a href='http://yahoo.com'>Visit Yahoo!</a>
    <form id='login' method='post' action='form.php'>
      <input name='name' type='text' value='jane'>
      <input type='submit'>
    </form>
    <img src='dad.jpg'>
  </body>
</html>
```

Starting with the <head> section, you can see that there are two elements. The first is the document's title of *Example*, contained within <title> and </title>

tags, whereas the second is the meta tag that tells search engine crawlers that the document may be crawled, its contents indexed, and any links can be followed:

```
<title>Example</title>
<meta name='robots' content='index, follow'>
```

This is done by passing the value `robots` to the name attribute and the string `index, follow` to the content attribute. Meta tags are self-closing (empty), so there is no `</meta>` tag. The section is then closed with a `</head>` tag:

```
</head>
```

Next is the body of the document, which is contained within `<body>` and `</body>` tags. There are three elements in this section: a link to *http://yahoo.com* in `<a>` and `</a>` tags, an embedded image that uses a self-closing `<img>` tag, and a form contained within `<form>` and `</form>` tags:

```
<body>
  <a href='http://yahoo.com'>Visit Yahoo!</a>
  <form id='login' method='post' action='form.php'>
    <input name='name' type='text' value='jane'>
    <input type='submit'>
  </form>
  <img src='dad.jpg'>
</body>
```

The form passes a value of `login` to the id attribute, `post` to the `method` attribute, and the program name `form.php` (the program that is to process the form data when it is submitted) is assigned to the `action` attribute, as follows (from now on, I will refer to the id attribute simply as an element's ID):

```
<form id='login' method='post' action='form.php'>
```

The method used for sending the data to the server is specified by the `method` attribute. Its value can be either `post` or `get`. This example uses a `post` request that sends the data in a hidden manner. (A `get` request would pass the posted data by attaching it after the URL in what is known as a *query string*.)

Inside the form there are two self-closing `<input>` tags. The first passes the string value name to the name attribute, `text` to the `type` attribute, and the value `jane` to the `value` attribute. This pre-populates the input field with the word `jane`, but it can be altered by the user:

```
<input name='name' type='text' value='jane'>
```

After this, a second `<input>` tag creates a submit button by passing the value `submit` to its `type` attribute:

```
<input type='submit'>
```

Finally, the form is closed with a `</form>` tag, and the image is displayed:

```
</form>
<img src='dad.jpg'>
```

When opened in a browser, the document looks something like Figure 15-2.

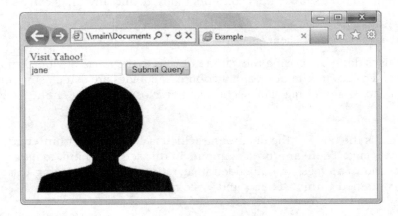

FIGURE 15-2 The result of displaying the example web page

Accessing the DOM from JavaScript

Now let's look at how elements can be manipulated from JavaScript, which (as you know) should always be placed within `<script>` and `</script>` tags, which these examples assume have already been applied. For example, the following code changes the document's title to An example web page:

```
document.title = 'An example web page'
```

As you will recall, JavaScript uses the period operator either to pass the current object to a function (or method) or to reference properties of objects. In this case, `title` is a property of the `document` object, so this statement has the same effect as if you opened the document in a program editor and directly edited the title within the `<title>` and `</title>` tags yourself.

Similarly, the form method type of `post` (in the example in the previous section) could be easily changed to `get`, like this:

```
document.forms.login.method = 'get'
```

Here the JavaScript references first the `document`, then the `forms` within that document, then the form with the ID of `login` and its `method`, which is then modified.

Using the `getElementById()` Function

In the previous couple of examples I showed you how to access parts of a document by their type, but there's a far, far easier method, which is to give every element in a document a unique ID, and then to access them from JavaScript using just those IDs.

For example, if the `<img>` tag is given an ID (such as `image1`) with which it can be identified, it's possible to replace the image loaded by it with another, as with the following code, in which the male-shaped dad.jpg image is replaced with mom.jpg to match the default name in the form field of jane:

```
<img src='dad.jpg' id='image1'>

<script>
  document.getElementById('image1').src = 'mom.jpg'
</script>
```

The trick here is to use the JavaScript function getElementById(), which will let you access any DOM element that has been given a unique ID. Therefore, let's look at another example by restoring the previous name and image mismatch by altering the default name value directly, rather than accessing the element via document.forms.login.

By giving the form field an ID (such as name) and using getElementById(), we can avoid the long-windedness of the previous example and go straight to the element to change it, like this (in which I have shown only the updated <input> tag HTML and not the remainder of the HTML—which remains unchanged):

```
<input name='name' type='text' value='jane' id='name'>

<script>
  document.getElementById('name').value = 'mike'
</script>
```

See how much easier it is than having to remember whether an element is part of a form, an image, or something else? All you have to do is know the ID of an element, and getElementById() will do the job of finding it for you.

Figure 15-3 shows how the web page now displays after these changes. The title is different, the default input value is mike, and the image shown is mom.jpg (yes, the gender is all confused again).

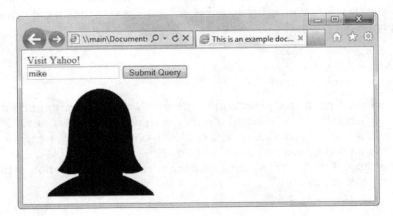

FIGURE 15-3   Three elements of the page have been modified with JavaScript.

The Simpler O() Function

I use the `getElementById()` function so often that I have created a simple function called O() (with an uppercase O) to make it quicker to type in. The function looks like this and I place it at the start of any JavaScript, right after the opening `<script>` tag, like this:

```
<script>
  function O(i)
  {
    return document.getElementById(i)
  }
</script>
```

Doing this saves 22 characters of typing each time the replacement O() function is used instead of the longer one.

One reason for the tremendous shortening is that the preceding `document.` has also been incorporated into the O() function, saving on typing in that too, as you can see if you compare the following long and short versions:

```
document.getElementById('name').value = 'mike'
O('name').value = 'mike'
```

However, there's one further step I like to take that makes the function even more useful and that's to allow the passing to it of either element IDs (which is what it does so far) or an object that has already been created (possibly as the result of previously having called the O() function).

Let me explain it like this. Instead of manipulating the `value` of the form input with the ID of name directly, let's first create an object from this element, like this:

```
newobject = O('name')
```

Now that I have this object, I can access it as often as I like without ever having to call the O() function again, like this, for example (in which the value is changed on separate occasions):

```
newobject.value = 'mike'
  // A few lines of code go here
newobject.value = 'fred'
```

However, I am a lazy programmer (as are all "good" programmers). Once I have created a function, I like to reuse it rather than writing a new one, and there are times when I would also like to pass either an object to the O() function (as you'll see in the following section) or an ID name.

Therefore, I prefer to use the following version of the function, which supports either type of argument:

```
function O(i)
{
  return typeof i == 'object' ? i : document.getElementById(i)
}
```

What is happening here is that the argument passed in i (for ID) is analyzed by the code, and if it happens to already be of the type object, the object is simply returned because it is already an object. But if it is not of that type, it is assumed to be an ID name, in which case it is looked up and returned as an object with a call to getElementById().

The Partner S() Function

In a similar fashion to the space saving produced by using the O() function, there is one other function that I use frequently because its action is also used all the time in JavaScript, and that's the new function S() (with an uppercase S). I use this to enable JavaScript to easily access any style attribute of any element.

For example, if I wish to change the width and height of the image, I can do it like this (which results in Figure 15-4, when the other lines of HTML and JavaScript we've been using are included):

```
<img src='mom.jpg' id='image1'>

<script>
  O('image1').style.width = '150px' // Longer syntax
  S('image1').height      = '120px' // Shorter syntax

  function O(i)
  {
    return typeof i == 'object' ? i : document.getElementById(i)
  }

  function S(i)
  {
    return O(i).style
  }
</script>
```

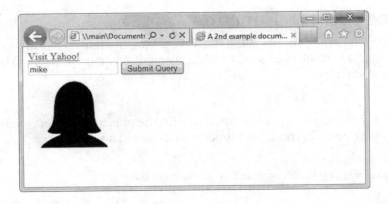

FIGURE 15-4   The *mom.jpg* image has been reduced in size.

What I've done here is simply make the S() function place a call to the O() function, but with an added .style suffix, and now I can use O() for accessing elements by name and S() for accessing the style attributes of elements by name.

What's more, because the O() function allows either ID names or objects, I can pass either type of argument to S() as well. Therefore, if I have an object called myobject (perhaps previously created using the O() function), I can change its width property like this:

```
S(myobject).width = '100px'
```

This code can be quicker, as the object is only looked up once, and is therefore a more efficient way to code when an element may be accessed more than once. This works because you are allowed to enter <script> tags as many times as you like in a document; there is no requirement to keep all your JavaScript code within a single set of <script> and </script> tags, although you may do so if you wish.

Accessing Multiple Elements by Class

So far I've provided you with two simple functions that make it easy for you to access any element on a web page and any style property of an element. Sometimes, though, you will want to access more than one element at a time and you can do this by assigning a CSS class name to each such element, like these examples:

```
<div class='MyClass'>Div contents</div>
<p class='MyClass'>Paragraph contents</p>
```

Then you can use the following handy C() (short for Class) function to return an array containing all the objects that match the class name provided:

```
function C(i)
{
  return document.getElementsByClassName(i)
}
```

Using the C() Function

To use the function, simply call it like this, saving the returned array so that you can access each of the elements individually as required or, more likely to be the case, en masse via a loop:

```
MyArray = C('MyClass')
```

Now you can do whatever you like with the objects returned, such as setting their textDecoration style property to underline, as follows:

```
for (i in MyArray)
  S(MyArray[i]).textDecoration = 'underline'
```

This code iterates through the objects in `MyArray[]` and then uses the `S()` function to reference each one's `style` property, setting its `textDecoration` property to `underline`, as shown by Figure 15-5.

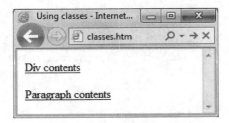

FIGURE 15-5   Modifying all elements in a class

The Difference Between Properties in CSS and JavaScript

Something important to note here is that the `textDecoration` property is an example of a CSS property that is normally hyphenated like this: `text-decoration`. But because JavaScript reserves the hyphen character for use as a mathematical operator, whenever you access a hyphenated CSS property, you must omit the hyphen and set the character immediately following it to uppercase. Another example of this is the `font-size` property, which is referenced in JavaScript as `fontSize` when placed after a period operator, like this:

```
MyObject.style.fontSize = '16pt'
```

Or like this if you are using my `S()` function:

```
S(MyObject).fontSize = '16pt'
```

The only possible alternative to this is to be more long-winded and use the `setAttribute()` function, which supports (and in fact requires) standard CSS property names, like this:

```
MyObject.setAttribute('style', 'font-size:16pt')
```

Note   Some versions of Microsoft Internet Explorer are picky about using the JavaScript-style CSS property names under specific conditions. So if you ever encounter problems with them, simply revert to the long form and use the `setAttribute()` function and you should be alright.

Summary of the Three Functions

Therefore, now you have three powerful functions you can use for quick and easy access of any individual web element (using `O()`), its `style` property (using `S()`), or a group of objects by class (using `C()`).

Together these will save you countless lines of programming code and speed up your development time substantially. Simply remember to copy the following into the section of any document you'll be accessing via JavaScript:

```
<script>
  function O(i)
  {
    return typeof i == 'object' ? i : document.getElementById(i)
  }

  function S(i)
  {
    return O(i).style
  }

  function C(i)
  {
    return document.getElementsByClassName(i)
  }
</script>
```

With this code pasted at the start of your web pages, JavaScript programming should be as easy as possible. Better still, instead of pasting them in, include the *mainfunctions.js* file supplied in the companion archive, like this:

```
<script src='mainfunctions.js'></script>
```

Just place that single line in the `<head>` of any web pages that access the functions.

Note   I use the functions `O()`, `S()`, and `C()` in the remainder of this book (as well as in all my other books and courses that cover JavaScript) because they substantially reduce the examples down in size, and also make them far easier for you to follow what's going on. Therefore, I assume you have included these functions at the start of your document as previously discussed and will not repeat their definitions in further examples.

Some Common Properties

Using JavaScript, you can modify any property of any element in a web document, in a similar manner to using CSS. I have already shown how to access CSS properties, using either the JavaScript short form or the `setAttribute()` function to use exact CSS property names. Therefore, I won't bore you by detailing all of these hundreds of properties.

Rather, I'd like to show you how to access just a few of the CSS properties as an overview of some of the things you can do.

First, then, let's look at modifying a few CSS properties from JavaScript using the following code, which first creates a <div> object, and then statements within a <script> section of HTML modify various attributes:

```
<div id='object'>Div Object</div>

<script>
  S('object').border     = 'solid 1px red'
  S('object').width      = '100px'
  S('object').height     = '100px'
  S('object').background = '#eee'
  S('object').color      = 'blue'
  S('object').fontSize   = '15pt'
  S('object').fontFamily = 'Helvetica'
  S('object').fontStyle  = 'italic'
</script>
```

Remember that this assumes you have included the set of three functions I provided earlier in the <head> of the web page first. Figure 15-6 shows the result of applying this code (available as *properties.htm* in the accompanying archive).

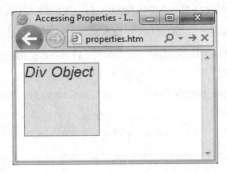

FIGURE 15-6   A <div> element with various properties modified

Other Properties

JavaScript also opens up access to a very wide range of other properties too, such as the width and height of the browser, and the same for any pop-up or in-browser windows or frames, and handy information such as the parent window (if there is one) and the history of URLs visited this session.

All these properties are accessed from the window object via the period operator (for example, window.name), and Table 15-1 lists them all, along with descriptions of each.

TABLE 15-1 Window Properties

Properties	Sets and/or Returns
closed	Returns a Boolean value indicating whether a window has been closed or not
defaultStatus	Sets or returns the default text in the status bar of a window
document	Returns the document object for the window
frames	Returns an array of all the frames and iframes in the window
history	Returns the history object for the window
innerHeight	Sets or returns the inner height of a window's content area
innerWidth	Sets or returns the inner width of a window's content area
length	Returns the number of frames and iframes in a window
location	Returns the location object for the window
name	Sets or returns the name of a window
navigator	Returns the navigator object for the window
opener	Returns a reference to the window that created the window
outerHeight	Sets or returns the outer height of a window, including tool and scroll bars
outerWidth	Sets or returns the outer width of a window, including tool and scroll bars
pageXOffset	Returns the pixels the document has been scrolled horizontally from the left of the window
pageYOffset	Returns the pixels the document has been scrolled vertically from the top of the window
parent	Returns the parent window of a window
screen	Returns the screen object for the window
screenLeft	Returns the x coordinate of the window relative to the screen (IE8 and below and all others browsers except Firefox)
screenTop	Returns the y coordinate of the window relative to the screen (IE8 and below and all others browsers except Firefox)
screenX	Returns the x coordinate of the window relative to the screen (IE9+ and all other browsers)
screenY	Returns the y coordinate of the window relative to the screen (IE9+ and all other browsers)
self	Returns the current window
status	Sets or returns the text in the status bar of a window
top	Returns the top browser window

There are a few points to note about some of these properties.

- The `defaultStatus` and `status` properties can be set only if users have modified their browsers to allow it (very unlikely).
- The `history` object cannot be read from (so you cannot see where your visitors have been surfing). However, it supports the `length` property to determine how long the history is, and the `back()`, `forward()`, and `go()` methods to navigate to specific pages in the history.
- When you need to know how much space is available in a current window of the web browser, just read the values in `window.innerHeight` and `window.innerWidth`—I often use these values for centering in-browser pop-up alerts or confirm dialog windows.
- The `screen` object supports the following read properties: `availHeight`, `availWidth`, `colorDepth`, `height`, `pixelDepth`, and `width`, and is therefore great for determining information about the user's display.

These few items of information will get you started and already provide you with many new and interesting things you can do with JavaScript. But, in fact, there are far more properties and methods available than can be covered in a crash course such as this. However, now that you know how to access and use properties, all you need is a resource listing them all, so I recommend you check out the following URL as a good initial point to start: *tinyurl.com/domproperties*.

Summary

Having become comfortable with working with the DOM in this lesson, you will now be able to easily access and modify most JavaScript elements and properties, either individually by ID name or as objects, or in groups by class names. You will also have added the three handy functions `O()`, `S()`, and `C()` to your programming toolkit to help with these things. In the following lesson we'll extend our rummaging through the DOM by inserting inline JavaScript and working directly with events.

Self-Test Questions

Using these questions, test how much you have learned in this lesson. If you don't know an answer, go back and reread the relevant section until your knowledge is complete. You can find the answers in Appendix A.

1. Which function is used to return an object based on an element's ID?

2. How can you modify a style property of an object?

3. Which function returns an array of objects for all elements of a specified type in a document?

4. How would you set the font size of the object MyObject to 12 points, using the setAttribute() function?

5. How can you achieve the same result as question 4 without using setAttribute()?

6. How can you determine how much space is available in the current window of the web browser?

7. How can you determine the width and height of the screen of the user's device?

8. How can you change the title of the current document from JavaScript?

9. In JavaScript, how can you change the image displayed by an <img> tag?

10. In JavaScript, how can you change the width and height of an image (or other element)?

Inserting Inline JavaScript and Events

To view the accompanying video for this lesson, please visit mhprofessional.com/ nixonjavascript/.

Sometimes the easiest way to achieve dynamic interaction with users of your web pages is to directly interact with them from the code they are using. So far we have mostly looked at running JavaScript from within `<script>` elements, but that is not the only way you can use it.

For example, it's quite legal to place JavaScript instructions inside elements, and you generally do this by attaching them to various event attributes such as `onmouseover`. What this does is enable you to provide interactivity to elements on an individual basis, and sometimes (if the task is simple enough) without even having to link it to functions later in a web document.

Therefore, tasks that might seem nontrivial, such as changing an image when the mouse passes over it, are easily achievable with a couple of simple JavaScript statements attached to the image. In this lesson you learn how this works, and also how to link to more complex code later in a web document should you wish to.

Also, in this lesson you will learn how you can even add new elements and remove existing ones from a document using JavaScript, providing an even greater level of flexibility and control.

Inline JavaScript

Using `<script>` tags isn't the only way you can execute JavaScript statements. You can also access JavaScript from within HTML tags, which makes for great dynamic interactivity.

For example, to add a quick effect when the mouse passes over an object, you can use the following HTML, which displays one image but replaces it with another when the mouse passes over:

```
<img src='dad.jpg'
  onmouseover="this.src='mom.jpg'"
    onmouseout="this.src='dad.jpg'">
```

Another Instance of `this`

In the preceding example, you see another instance of the `this` keyword in use, where it tells JavaScript to operate on the calling object, namely the `<img>` tag. You can see the result in the top half of Figure 16-1, created using the file *inline.htm* from the companion archive—try it for yourself and you'll see how the *mom.jpg* image swaps in and out as you pass your mouse over the *dad.jpg* image (although you won't see anything changing in this figure, you will if you try this example in your browser).

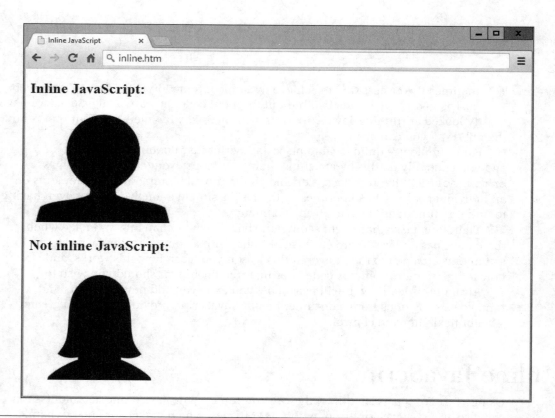

FIGURE 16-1 Applying JavaScript to HTML tag events

Non-inline Event Attaching

The preceding code is the equivalent of providing an ID to the `<img>` tag, and then attaching the actions to the tag's mouse events, like this:

```
<img id='object' src='dad.jpg'>

<script>
  O('object').onmouseover = function()
    { this.src = 'mom.jpg' }
  O('object').onmouseout = function()
    { this.src = 'dad.jpg' }
</script>
```

This code applies the `id` of `object` to the tag in the HTML section and then proceeds to manipulate it separately in the JavaScript section by attaching anonymous functions to each event.

Note Any of the preceding methods are fine for attaching to element events, and the one you use is entirely up to you. However, I would personally reserve the first style (inline JavaScript) just for popping in quick bits of interactivity here and there, and would normally use the second (separate JavaScript) when I am writing a lot of code. I do this because when programs get larger, I like all the code to be in the same place where I can work on it independently from the HTML. It also separates the code from the content so that I can easily go in and change the event actions in the JavaScript section, without touching the HTML.

Attaching to Other Events

Using either inline or separate JavaScript, you find several events to which you can attach actions, providing a wealth of additional features you can make available for your users. Table 16-1 lists some of these events, and details when they will be triggered.

Note You can attach to these events in either previously described manner, but make sure you attach events to objects that make sense. For example, an object that is not a form will not respond to the `onsubmit` event.

Adding New Elements

With JavaScript you are not limited to only manipulating the elements and objects supplied to a document in its HTML. In fact, you can create objects at will by inserting them into the Document Object Model (DOM). For example, suppose you need a new `<div>` element. Here's one way you can add it to the web page:

```
newdiv = document.createElement('div')
document.body.appendChild(newdiv)
```

TABLE 16-1 Events and When They Are Triggered

Event	Occurs
onabort	When an image's loading is stopped before completion
onblur	When an element loses focus
onchange	When the value of the element has changed
onclick	When an object is clicked
ondblclick	When an object is double-clicked
onerror	When a JavaScript error is encountered
onfocus	When an element gets focus
onkeydown	When a key is being pressed (inc. SHIFT, ALT, CTRL, and ESC)
onkeypress	When a key is pressed (not SHIFT, ALT, CTRL, and ESC)
onkeyup	When a key is released
onload	When an object has loaded
onmousedown	When the mouse button is pressed over an element
onmousemove	When the mouse is moved over an element
onmouseout	When the mouse leaves an element
onmouseover	When the mouse passes over an element from outside it
onmouseup	When the mouse button is released
onsubmit	When a form is submitted
onreset	When a form is reset
onresize	When the browser is resized
onscroll	When the document is scrolled
onselect	When some text is selected
onunload	When a document is removed

First, the new element is created with createElement(), but it isn't yet inserted into the DOM and so won't be displayed. Then the appendChild() function is called, and the element gets inserted into the DOM and therefore is displayed.

Figure 16-2 shows this code (*addelement.htm* in the companion archive) being used to add a new <div> element to a web document. This new element is exactly the same as if it had been included in the original HTML, and has all the same properties and methods available.

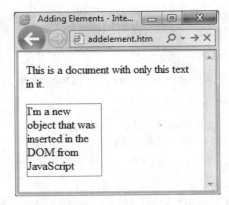

FIGURE 16-2   Adding a `<div>` to a web page

I sometimes use this method when I want to create in-browser pop-up windows because it doesn't need a spare `<div>` to be available in the DOM.

Removing Elements

You can also remove elements from the DOM, including ones that you didn't insert using JavaScript. It's just as easy as adding an element and works like this, assuming the element to remove is in the object `element`:

```
element.parentNode.removeChild(element)
```

This code accesses the element's `parentNode` object so that it can remove the element from that node. Then it calls the `removeChild()` method on that object, passing the object to be removed.

Alternatives to Adding and Removing Elements

Inserting an element is intended for adding major new objects into a web page. But if all you are doing is hiding and revealing objects according to an `onmouseover` or other event, don't forget that there are always a couple of CSS properties you can use for this purpose, without taking such drastic measures as creating and deleting DOM elements.

For example, when you want to make an element invisible but leave it in place (and with all the elements surrounding it remaining in their positions), you can simply set the object's `visibility` property to `hidden`, like this:

```
MyObject.style.visibility = 'hidden'
```

And to redisplay the object, you can use the following:

```
MyObject.style.visibility = 'visible'
```

You can also collapse elements down to occupy zero width and height (with all objects around it filling in the freed-up space) like this:

```
MyObject.style.display = 'none'
```

To then restore an element to its original dimensions, you would use the following:

```
MyObject.style.display = 'block'
```

If you prefer, you can also use the shorter S() function from *mainfunctions.js* in the companion archive of files, like this:

```
S(MyObject).display = 'block'
```

 While you're at it, don't forget other great CSS properties you can access from JavaScript, such as `opacity` for setting the visibility of an object to somewhere between visible and invisible, or simply changing the `width` and `height` properties of an object to resize it. And, of course, using the `position` property with values of `absolute`, `static`, or `relative`, you can even locate an object anywhere in the browser window that you like.

Controlling HTML5 Media

For the last few years, since the dawn of HTML5, it has been possible to embed audio and video into web browsers without needing plug-ins. Things started off a little slow with varied browser take-up. And then there were a few skirmishes about which audio and video software to use, meaning that media had to be converted into a few different formats to work on all browsers. But nowadays a couple of formats will suffice for all major browsers, and embedding media in a web page is really simple.

In fact, you don't even need JavaScript to add audio or video to a web page, but once the audio or video is embedded, you can provide greater functionality by attaching JavaScript to it to create your own methods of playing or pausing playback and so on.

Adding audio or video to a web page is as simple as using either the <audio> or the <video> tag, and then supplying one or more <source> tags to tell the web browser where to fetch the media from. For example, here's some HTML to add audio to a web page, which results in Figure 16-3:

```
<!DOCTYPE html>
<html>
  <head>
    <title>HTML5 Audio</title>
    <style>
      #player { margin:40px; display:block; }
    </style>
  </head>
```

```
<body>
  <audio controls>
    <source src='audio.m4a' type='audio/aac'>
    <source src='audio.mp3' type='audio/mpeg'>
    <source src='audio.ogg' type='audio/ogg'>
  </audio>
</body>
</html>
```

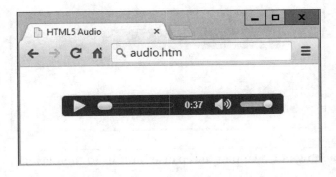

FIGURE 16-3   Playing an audio file with HTML5

In the `<audio>` section there are three files, all containing the same audio, but converted to AAC, MP3, and OGG. Because of the `controls` attribute, the audio player is shown; otherwise, it would not display and there would be no way to play the audio (unless it was set to auto start, which can be very annoying).

However, if we give the `<audio>` element an ID (such as `player`), we can then attach to it with JavaScript to create our own (in this case, very simple) play and pause buttons. Here's all we have to do (the result of which is shown in Figure 16-4):

```
<!DOCTYPE html>
<html>
  <head>
    <title>HTML5 Audio</title>
    <script src='mainfunctions.js'></script>
    <style>
      #player { margin:40px; display:block; }
    </style>
  </head>
  <body>
    <audio controls id='player'>
      <source src='audio.m4a' type='audio/aac'>
      <source src='audio.mp3' type='audio/mpeg'>
      <source src='audio.ogg' type='audio/ogg'>
    </audio>
```

```
        <button onclick="O('player').play()">Play</button>
        <button onclick="O('player').pause()">Pause</button>
    </body>
</html>
```

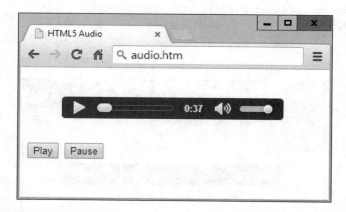

FIGURE 16-4   Attaching our own play and pause buttons to the player

Two new buttons have been added underneath the audio player, and the *mainfunctions.js* file has been included within the `<head>` section to give access to the `O()` function. Using `O()`, you attach the HTML5 `play()` and `pause()` functions to the `onclick` events of the two new buttons, and can now possibly remove the `controls` attribute from the `<audio>` tag if you wish to remove the default player from view.

So, our new interface isn't very pretty, but now that you see how this works, you can attach the controls you need to any interface of your design. And you can do exactly the same with HTML5 video too, like this (see Figure 16-5):

```
<!DOCTYPE html>
<html>
  <head>
    <title>HTML5 Video</title>
    <script src='mainfunctions.js'></script>
    <style>
      #player { margin:40px; display:block; }
    </style>
  </head>
  <body>
    <video width='560' height='320' id='player' controls>
      <source src='video.mp4'  type='video/mp4' >
      <source src='video.webm' type='video/webm'>
      <source src='video.ogv'  type='video/ogg' >
    </video>
```

```
        <button onclick="O('player').play()">Play</button>
        <button onclick="O('player').pause()">Pause</button>
    </body>
</html>
```

FIGURE 16-5   Embedding HTML5 video with attached play and pause buttons

Summary

Having now learned numerous ways of interacting with web pages using the DOM, the things you can do with JavaScript are now limited only by your imagination. In Lesson 17, I'll show you a few more advanced things you can do, starting with how to use cookies and access the local storage made available with HTML5.

Self-Test Questions

Using these questions, test how much you have learned in this lesson. If you don't know an answer, go back and reread the relevant section until your knowledge is complete. You can find the answers in Appendix A.

1. How would you change the file displayed by an `<img>` tag to *newimage.jpg* when the mouse passes over it?

2. Which event is triggered when an element is clicked?

3. With which function can you create a new element?

4. With which function can you attach a newly created element to the DOM?

5. How can you remove an element from the DOM?

6. How can you change the visibility of an object?

7. How can you prevent an object from displaying at all (without even reserving the space it should occupy)?

8. With which functions can you stop and restart HTML5 audio and video playback?

9. To which element(s) should you attach the functions referred to in question 8?

10. How can you specify whether or not the default play and other buttons display on an audio or video player?

Controlling Cookies and Local Storage

 To view the accompanying video for this lesson, please visit mhprofessional.com/ nixonjavascript/.

Your journey to become a master JavaScript programmer is progressing well, and you will now be able to write a wide variety of programs, but there are still quite a few more things you need to know before you become fully proficient in the language.

For example, web developers need a way to keep track of users to their websites, and historically this has generally been achieved through the use of cookies. Therefore, in this lesson I show you how to manage cookies from JavaScript, and I also introduce the newer and more powerful HTML5 feature called *local storage*.

Using Cookies

Cookies (the nonedible kind) are those little snippets of data that get saved on your computer and that everyone makes such a fuss about because some companies use them to track your surfing and buying habits. However, cookies are extremely useful and, in fact, invaluable for making your users' visits to your web pages as smooth and enjoyable as possible.

You see, cookies are used by sites like Facebook and Twitter to keep you logged in so that you can keep going back without having to continually reenter your username and login details. And now I will show you how easy it is for you to set and read cookies using JavaScript, so that you can provide the same functionality.

To create a cookie, you simply assign it a value that contains the various details it needs to store on the user's computer. These include the cookie name, its contents, its expiry date, the domain to which it applies, the path to the server issuing it, and whether it is secure or not. This may sound complicated, but look at the following (which I have split over two lines to avoid word wrapping at unexpected characters):

```
document.cookie =
  'username=fredsmith; expires=Mon, 31 Dec 2018 23:59:59 UTC'
```

The cookie set by this assignment has the name `username` and the value `fredsmith`, and it will stay on the user's computer (unless manually removed) until midnight on New Year's Eve 2018 UTC (Universal Coordinated Time)—which is practically the same as GMT (Greenwich Mean Time), the time in London, England (without summer time, or daylight saving time).

However, it's actually a little more complicated than that because to be able to store values in cookies such as special characters and spaces, they need to be run through the JavaScript `encodeURI()` function, which turns the unusual characters into escape sequences. Plus, I haven't yet shown you how to set a cookie's path, domain, and security.

Setting a Cookie

Therefore, let me provide you with a function you can use that will do all of these for you, including converting special characters to escape sequences:

```
function SetCookie(name, value, seconds, path, domain, secure)
{
  var date = new Date()
  date.setTime(date.getTime() + seconds * 1000)

  var expires      = seconds ? ';expires=' + date.toGMTString() : ''
  path             = path    ? ';path='    + path               : ''
  domain           = domain  ? ';domain='  + domain             : ''
  secure           = secure  ? ';secure'                        : ''
  document.cookie = name + '=' + encodeURI(value) +
    expires + path + domain + secure
}
```

If you use this function whenever you must set a cookie, all you need to think about is the arguments to pass to it, which are as follows:

- **name**   The cookie's name.
- **value**   The cookie's value.
- **seconds** (Optional)   The number of seconds until cookie expiry.
- **path** (Optional)   The path to the issuing server.
- **domain** (Optional)   The web domain to use.
- **secure** (Optional)   If "secure", the browser must use SSL.

The name and value arguments are quite clear, and now setting the optional expiry date is easier because you simply specify the number of seconds in the future before it should expire. Therefore, for example, for a month's time, it would be 60 seconds × 60 minutes × 24 hours × 30 days, which gives a value of 2592000 seconds, so just supply that number as the argument value for seconds.

Regarding the optional path argument, this should generally either be left as ' ', not supplied, or you should choose a value of / so that the cookie will be accessible across all directories on the server. However, if you really need to restrict it to a certain subdirectory, such as /login/, then specify that instead.

The same goes for the optional domain argument. Generally, you can leave this as ' ' or not supply it and the cookie will work on the entire domain of the website (such as *mysite.com*). Or if you need to, you can specify a subdomain of your website such as *subdomain.mysite.com* to restrict access to the cookie to that domain only.

Finally, if you have a secure web server running and wish to restrict cookie exchanges to use the Secure Socket Layer (SSL) protocol, usually via HTTPS (HyperText Transfer Protocol Secure), then set the optional secure argument to true; otherwise (as is usually the case), don't pass the argument, or set it to false.

Therefore, to make a call to only set a cookie's value and expiry (leaving all other settings at their default values), you might issue a simple statement such as this:

```
SetCookie('username', 'fredsmith', 2592000)
```

Reading a Cookie

Reading back a cookie's value can also be a little tricky because all the cookies are stored in the single document.cookie string, so here's another function you can use to extract individual cookies from the string:

```
function GetCookie(name)
{
  var dc    = ';' + document.cookie
  var start = dc.indexOf(';' + name + '=')

  if (start == -1) return false

  start  += name.length + 2
  var end = dc.indexOf(';', start)
  end     = (end == -1) ? dc.length : end

  return decodeURI(dc.substring(start, end))
}
```

This function first places a ; character before the document.cookie property and places the result in dc. This is because all cookies must end with a semicolon (which therefore must mark the start of the next one), and so searching for the start of a cookie is easily achieved by looking for `;cookiename`. However, the first cookie will not have a `;` in front of it, so we prepend one to allow all instances to be searched.

The function then searches for the value in `name` (but prepended with a `;` character, and followed by `=`) to see whether a cookie of that value exists, and returns `false` if not.

If a cookie name is matched, the cookie's value is then read by extracting the string immediately following the `=` character up to the next `;` character, which contains the *value* part of the *key* = *value* string. Any escape sequences are returned to special characters, and the result is returned. To read back a cookie you have saved on a user's computer, you can use a statement such as this:

```
username = GetCookie('username')
```

The variable `username` will now either have the value `false` if the cookie was not found or it will contain the cookie's value.

Deleting a Cookie

To delete a cookie, I have provided one further function you can call to also save you from having to write your own (even though it's actually quite straightforward) as follows:

```
function DeleteCookie(name)
{
  SetCookie(name, '', -3600)
}
```

This function simply saves a cookie of the name in `name` with no value, and sets its expiry to −3600 seconds (1 hour in the past), whose result is that the cookie expires. To delete a cookie, therefore, you use a statement such as this:

```
DeleteCookie('username')
```

These three functions are saved for you in the file *cookiefunctions.js* in the accompanying archive so that you can include them in your code as required. Figure 17-1 shows them being tested in the accompanying file *cookies.htm* (also from the companion archive), with an alert window displaying the current value of a cookie.

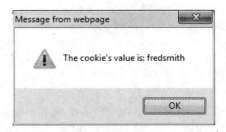

FIGURE 17-1 Setting and reading a cookie

Once you've set a cookie for a user, the next time he or she returns to your website, just check for the existence of that cookie, and if it has a value, you can use it to look up their details and personalize your content for them. You can store passwords and other values in cookies too, and the reasonable 4-K size limit per domain of the document .cookie string means you can probably store all the cookies you could want.

If other people will have access to a user's computer, they could possibly discover a password saved in a cookie by examining their cookies in the browser or an external cookie file, so it is preferable to use some kind of identifier that is not their password but that can identify the user to your web server and that you then immediately change to another value after reading it so that such values cannot be reused, as they are only ever temporary. Also, saving and reading cookies may not always work on a local file system on all browsers. If you intend to test these functions to be sure they will work, you may need to try them out on a web server using an `http://` address, not a `file://` address.

Using Local Storage

If you need to store much larger amounts of data than is possible with cookies, you can try saving them in the user's HTML5 local storage space, which supports at least 2.5MB and up to 10MB per domain, depending on the browser.

To access local storage, you use methods of the `localStorage` object such as `setItem()`, `getItem()`, `removeItem()`, and `clear()`. For example, to locally store a user's username and password, you might use code such as this:

```
localStorage.setItem('username', 'Alice')
localStorage.setItem('password', 'MyPassword;#!')
```

If the size of the value is larger than the disk quota remaining for the storage area, an "Out of memory" exception is thrown. Otherwise, when another page loads or when the user returns to the website, these details can be retrieved to save the user entering them again, like this:

```
username = localStorage.getItem('username')
password = localStorage.getItem('password')
```

If the key doesn't exist, the `getItem()` function returns a value of `null`. You don't have to use these function names if you don't want to, and can access the `localStorage` object directly, because the two following statements are equivalent to each other:

```
localStorage.setItem('key', 'value')
localStorage['key'] = 'value'
```

And the two following statements are therefore also equivalent to each other:

```
value = localStorage.getItem('key')
value = localStorage['key']
```

Figure 17-2 shows an `alert()` message window displaying these values being retrieved from local storage, using the following code:

```
if (typeof localStorage == 'undefined')
{
  document.write("Local storage unavailable.")
}
else
{
  document.write("Local storage available.")

  localStorage.setItem('username', 'Alice')
  localStorage.setItem('password', 'MyPassword;#!')

  username = localStorage.getItem('username')
  password = localStorage.getItem('password')

  alert("Data retrieved: username = '" + username +
    "', password = '" + password + "'.")
}
```

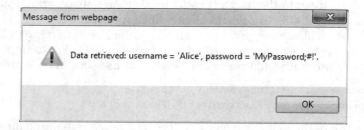

FIGURE 17-2   Values have been retrieved from local storage.

The first part of code within the `if()` statement writes an error message to the web page if local storage is not supported in the browser. This is determined by examining the `localStorage` object and, if it is undefined, local storage is unavailable. In the `else` part of the code, a message is first written to the web page indicating that local storage is supported. Then the `username` and `password` are saved to local storage with the `setItem()` function.

Next, these values are retrieved from local storage into the variables `username` and `password`. Finally, an `alert()` message window is popped up that displays the retrieved values.

Until they are erased, these values will remain in the local storage once saved, and you can verify this by trying the preceding code for yourself (saved as *localstorage.htm* in the companion archive), running it once, commenting out the two lines of code that call `setItem()`, and then running it again—the alert window will still report the same vales.

Removing and Clearing Local Data

To remove an item of data from the local storage, all you need to do is issue a command such as this:

```
localStorage.removeItem('username')
```

This deletes the item from local storage. You can also completely clear the local storage for the current domain by issuing this command:

```
localStorage.clear()
```

 Try any of these methods on the preceding example and run it again, and you'll find that the values have been erased.

Summary

Using the information you have learned in this lesson, you will now be able to provide personalization to your websites to make your users feel right at home. If, for example, the site requires a username and password to participate, once these details have been entered one time, you can store them in cookies and automatically keep the person logged in until they choose to log out.

You now also have the ability to save large amounts of data in a user's local storage space. How you use it is up to you, but you could, for example, support creating and storing memos, to-do lists, and other information locally, making it possible to create web apps that can be run offline without requiring access to a web server for storing data.

In Lesson 18 we'll look at how you can further accommodate your users by tailoring their browsing experience to their particular browser.

Self-Test Questions

Using these questions, test how much you have learned in this lesson. If you don't know an answer, go back and reread the relevant section until your knowledge is complete. You can find the answers in Appendix A.

1. Which DOM property holds cookie values?

2. How can you create a new cookie?

3. How can you read a cookie's value?

4. How can you delete a cookie?

5. What is the purpose of the `domain` argument for cookie storage?

6. How can you test whether a browser supports local storage?

7. How can you save an item of data to local storage?

8. How can you read an item of data from local storage?

9. How can you remove an item of data from local storage?

10. How can you empty all local storage for the current domain?

Working with Different Browsers

To view the accompanying video for this lesson, please visit mhprofessional.com/ nixonjavascript/.

In the beginning there was the Mosaic web browser and all web pages displayed the same. Then along came Netscape Navigator and there were now two competing standards. Microsoft wasn't happy about this and so it also released a browser called *Internet Explorer* (IE), which made web developing something you had to do three times to ensure your sites looked good on all browsers. However, because Microsoft gave the browser away, it effectively killed off the other two browsers, and so compatibility stopped being an issue and the world of web developing settled down for a few years.

But then there came the descendant of Netscape, Mozilla Firefox, which made rapid inroads into the market share of IE because it was fast and slick and had many new features. And, because it approached things from a different point of view, web pages started to look different again on different browsers.

At the same time, other browsers such as Opera and Safari entered the fray, followed by the likes of Google Chrome, and then the iOS and Android browsers. Fortunately, though, all the new browsers tended to agree with the W3C (Worldwide Web Consortium) on how HTML should be handled, so most of the incompatibilities were considered by developers to be the fault of IE. Therefore, code generally would be written once for non-IE browsers, and then had to be tweaked (often a considerable process on a large site) to run the same on IE.

However, because of the overwhelming support of competing browsers causing IE to lose market share, over the last couple of iterations, Internet Explorer has become faster, more sophisticated, and ever more compatible with the industry standards. Therefore, now we find ourselves back in a position where developers can spend most of their time simply designing, and not so much catering for inconsistencies.

Nevertheless, browsers are massively powerful applications packed with hundreds of thousands of lines of complex code, and there will probably always be a few differences between major browsers, and as a developer you need to have a way to distinguish between browsers (and even versions of browsers) to tailor your code where necessary. In this lesson I show you how to do just that, as well as how to read and make use of the query string (the alphanumeric data that is often attached to URLs).

The User Agent String

Every web page request has a user agent string passed with it by well-behaved browsers. You can usually rely on this string to determine information about the user's computer and web browser. However, some browsers allow the user to modify the user agent string, and some web spiders and other "bots" use misleading user agents, or even don't provide any user agent string.

Nevertheless, on the whole, it is a very handy item of data to make use of, and takes a form such as the formidable following user agent string:

```
Mozilla/5.0 (compatible; MSIE 10.0; Windows NT 6.1; Trident/4.0; InfoPath.2;
 SV1; .NET CLR 2.0.50727; WOW64)
```

Each string can be different from any other due to the way the browser is configured, its brand and version, the add-ons in it, the operating system used, and so on. In the instance of the preceding string, it states that the browser is Internet Explorer 10, it is broadly compatible with version 5 of Mozilla-based browsers such as Firefox, the operating system is Windows 7 (NT 6.1), the layout engine is Trident, .NET framework 2.0.50727 is running on the computer, and the browser is a Windows-On-Windows program (a 32-bit application running on a 64-bit processor).

Most of these you can normally ignore, but the most useful piece of information is that the browser is Internet Explorer, because sometimes you need to tailor code to specific browsers, and most frequently that has been the case with Internet Explorer because of a history of incorporating nonstandard features.

The `GetBrowser()` Function

To extract this information from the user agent string, you can use a function such as the following, which checks a couple of other useful properties as well as `userAgent`:

```
function GetBrowser()
{
  var agent

  if      (document.all)             agent = 'IE'
  else if (window.opera)             agent = 'Opera'
  else if (NavCheck('Trident'))      agent = 'IE'
  else if (NavCheck('OPR'))          agent = 'Opera'
  else if (NavCheck('Chrome'))       agent = 'Chrome'
  else if (NavCheck('iPod'))         agent = 'iPod'
  else if (NavCheck('iPhone'))       agent = 'iPhone'
  else if (NavCheck('iPad'))         agent = 'iPad'
  else if (NavCheck('Android'))      agent = 'Android'
```

```
    else if (NavCheck('Safari'))   agent = 'Safari'
    else if (NavCheck('Gecko'))    agent = 'Firefox'
    else                           agent = 'Unknown'

    return agent

    function NavCheck(check)
    {
      return navigator.userAgent.indexOf(check) != -1
    }
}
```

This code determines whether the browser is an early version of Internet Explorer by checking the document.all property, which exists only in IE. Then it interrogates window.opera to see whether the browser is an early version of Opera. After that, the user agent string is tested for all major browsers such as newer versions of Opera and IE, as well as Google Chrome, Apple Safari, Mozilla Firefox, Google Android, and various Apple iOS devices.

The command that interrogates the user agent string is the following, which uses the indexOf() function to find out whether the value in check is contained in userAgent (returning true if so):

```
return navigator.userAgent.indexOf(check) != -1
```

Using the Function

You can copy this function into your own code and simply make a call such as the following to assign the current browser name to the variable Browser:

```
Browser = GetBrowser()
```

Figure 18-1 shows this function being called using the *useragent.htm* file from the companion archive.

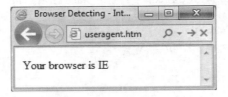

FIGURE 18-1   Returning the current browser name

 Did you notice how the NavCheck() function was placed inside the GetBrowser() function? This is because it is called only by that function and so putting it in the function keeps the code tidy and easy to follow. However, if your code ever needs to call the NavCheck() function directly, you should move it back outside again.

The Query String

The query string is the part of a URL that follows the document file name and is preceded with a ? character. Typically, it is used to send Get requests from a form to a web server. A Get request is one where all the data being sent to the sever is in clear view (as opposed to a Post request that sends the data invisibly, attaching nothing to the URL).

A typical URL with a Get request might look like the following search request made to the Google search engine:

```
http://www.google.com/search?q=query+string&ie=utf-8
```

The query string here is the part after the ?, as follows:

```
q=query+string&ie=utf-8
```

In this instance, the query string has two key/value pairs (separated by the & character):

```
q = query+string
ie = utf-8
```

 Query strings are almost always escaped so that any special characters are replaced with escape characters, and in this instance, the space character has become a + character (but could have also been encoded as %20 like in q=query%20 string).

The `GetQueryString()` Function

However, it isn't only web servers that can process Get requests, because you can read query strings from JavaScript too, using a function such as this:

```
function GetQueryString()
{
  var parts = window.location.search.substr(1).split('&')

  for (var i in parts)
    parts[i] = parts[i].split('=')

  return p
}
```

This function accesses the query string in `window.location.search`. But because a ? character is always included (even though it's not actually part of the query string), the `substr()` function is called with an argument of 1, which passes on everything but the first character to the `split()` function:

```
var parts = window.location.search.substr(1).split('&')
```

The `split()` function then splits the string at all occurrences of &, placing the parts into the array `parts`. Then a `for()` loop iterates through the parts, separating each into key/value pairs by splitting them at occurrences of the = character. The string value in parts[i] is then replaced with an array containing the key in its first element and the value in its second element:

```
for (var i in parts)
  parts[i] = parts[i].split('=')
```

Finally, the parts array is returned:

```
return parts
```

Using the Function

To obtain the keys and values in the query string, all your code has to do is call this function as follows:

```
Query = GetQueryString()
```

The array Query will now contain an array of key/value pairs, with each key and value stored in a sub-array for each element. Therefore, you can iterate through the array, for example, like this (liberally whitespaced for clarity):

```
for (i in Query)
  document.write(Query[i][0] + ' = ' +
                 Query[i][1] + '<br>')
```

Because query strings have escaped values, when you actually want to use a key or value, you will need to decode it like this:

```
Key0 = decodeURIComponent(Query[0][0])
Val0 = decodeURIComponent(Query[0][1])
```

These lines assign the first key and its value to Key0 and Val0, first putting them through the decodeURIComponent() function. The second key and value (if any) could be extracted like this (and so on):

```
Key1 = decodeURIComponent(Query[1][0])
Val1 = decodeURIComponent(Query[1][1])
```

Figure 18-2 shows a query string of ?a=1&b=2 appended to the example file *query.htm* (from the companion archive). If you wish to test this file, remember to add that string to the end of the URL in the address bar, like this:

```
query.htm?a=1&b=2
```

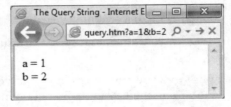

FIGURE 18-2   Reading and displaying query string values

You may sometimes see the deprecated unescape() function used instead of decodeURIComponent(). But unescape() is in the process of being dropped, so you should use decodeURIComponent() instead to ensure future compatibility for your code.

Summary

Now that you know how to determine the browser that is running your code, you have the ability to modify your pages accordingly. For example, on a device that has a phone included such as an iPhone or Android phone, you could highlight any phone numbers to make them easily selectable. Or you can reformat the layout of a website to better fit a much smaller screen.

You can now also read the contents of query strings to see whether visitors have come to your web page from a particular search engine, and can also modify your display accordingly, perhaps by highlighting any keywords that were searched for.

Therefore, now that you have all the basics of JavaScript web development under your belt, in the remaining pair of lessons, we'll move on to some advanced (but fun) programming that will really make your websites stand out from the crowd, starting with implementing interrupt-driven code.

Self-Test Questions

Using these questions, test how much you have learned in this lesson. If you don't know an answer, go back and reread the relevant section until your knowledge is complete. You can find the answers in Appendix A.

1. What is the best way to test whether a browser is Internet Explorer?

2. What is the best way to test whether a browser is Opera?

3. With which object can you test for all other browser types?

4. What is a query string?

5. What character immediately precedes a query string in a URL?

6. Which character separates key/value pairs in a query string?

7. How is a space character represented in a query string?

8. Which property contains the current query string?

9. With which function can you separate key=value substrings from a query string into an array?

10. Given an array of key=value substrings, how can you turn each string element into a sub-array containing the key in its first element and value in its second element?

19

Implementing Interrupts and Timeouts

To view the accompanying video for this lesson, please visit mhprofessional.com/ nixonjavascript/.

To allow computers to do more than one thing at a time, they use a technique called *interrupts,* in which each process is given a few cycles of processor time in turn. At any one time only one process is active, but because the computer switches between them really quickly, they appear to be all running simultaneously.

Apart from supporting multitasking, interrupts are perfect for cutting down on unresponsive behavior. For example, if you have to wait while a program does something such as fetch some data from a web server, it can be very annoying, but with timeouts, a task can be initiated, which then runs under interrupts as a background program, to then report back when it has completed, leaving you or the foreground task to get on with the current work in hand.

JavaScript supports both types of interrupts, enabling you to run multiple programs at a time, and to pass off tasks to programs to complete in the background, and it's all actually quite easy to implement.

Using Interrupts

JavaScript provides access to interrupts, a method by which you can ask the browser to call your code after a set period of time, or even to keep calling it at specified intervals. This provides you with a means of handling background tasks such as Ajax (Asynchronous JavaScript And XML) communications (covered next), or even things like animating web elements.

To accomplish this, there are two types of interrupts, `setTimeout()` and `setInterval()`, both of which have the accompanying functions `clearTimeout()` and `clearInterval()` for turning them off again.

Using `setTimeout()`

When you call `setTimeout()`, you pass it some JavaScript code or the name of a function and the value in milliseconds representing how long to wait before the code should be executed, like this:

```
setTimeout(DoThis, 5000)
```

And your `DoThis()` function might look like this:

```
function DoThis()
{
  alert('This is your wakeup alert!')
}
```

Figure 19-1 shows this code (saved as *settimeout.htm* in the companion archive) being loaded into a browser.

FIGURE 19-1   The alert pops up after the specified delay.

In case you are wondering, you cannot simply supply the `alert()` function as a `setTimeout()` argument because the `alert()` would be executed immediately. Only when you provide either an anonymous function or a function name without parentheses can you safely pass that function to be called later.

Passing a String

There is an exception to this, though, because you can pass a string value to the setTimeout() function, and then it will not be executed until the correct time, like this:

```
setTimeout("alert('Hello!')", 5000)
```

In fact, you can place as many lines of JavaScript code as you like, if you place a semicolon after each statement, like this (saved as *settimeout2.htm* in the accompanying archive):

```
setTimeout("document.write('Starting'); alert('Hello!')", 5000)
```

 I tend to prefer using separate functions in interrupts so that I can modify the function if necessary, without having to alter the code that generates the interrupt.

Repeating Timeouts

One technique some programmers use to provide repeating interrupts with setTimeout() is to call the setTimeout() function from the code called by it, as with the following, which will initiate a never-ending loop of alert windows:

```
setTimeout(DoThis, 5000)

function DoThis()
{
  setTimeout(DoThis, 5000)
  alert('I am annoying!')
}
```

Now the alert will pop up every 5 seconds, so if you try out this code (*settimeout3 .htm* in the accompanying archive), you'll need to click the Home button in your browser to snap out of the loop.

Cancelling a Timeout

Once a timeout has been set up, you cannot cancel it unless you previously saved the value returned from the initial call to setTimeout(), like this:

```
handle = setTimeout(DoThis, 5000)
```

Armed with the value in handle, you can now cancel the interrupt at any point up until its due time, like this:

```
clearTimeout(handle)
```

When you do this, the interrupt is completely forgotten about and the code assigned to it will not get executed. The file *cleartimeout.htm* in the accompanying archive illustrates this in action.

Using `setInterval()`

An easier way to set up regular interrupts is to use the `setInterval()` function. It works in just the same way, except that after popping up after the interval you specify in milliseconds, it will do so again after that interval passes, and so on forever, unless you cancel it.

Let's use this function to display a simple clock in the browser, like this (using liberal whitespace for neat layout):

```
function ShowTime(object)
{
  var date = new Date()

  object.innerHTML = date.toTimeString().substr(0, 8)
}
```

Every time `ShowTime()` is called, it sets the object `date` to the current date and time with a call to `Date()`:

```
var date = new Date()
```

Then the `innerHTML` property of the object passed to `ShowTime()` (namely `object`) is set to the current time in hours, minutes, and seconds, as determined by a call to `toTimeString()`. This returns a string such as `09:17:12 UTC+0530`, which is then truncated to just the first eight characters with a call to the `substr()` function:

```
object.innerHTML = date.toTimeString().substr(0, 8)
```

Using `ShowTime()`

To use this function, you first have to create an object whose `innerHTML` property will be used for displaying the time, like this HTML:

```
The time is: <span id='time'>00:00:00</span>
```

Then, from a `<script>` section of code, all you have to do is place a call to the `setInterval()` function, like this:

```
setInterval("ShowTime(O('time'))", 1000)
```

This statement assumes you have loaded in the O() function by including the *mainfunctions.js* file. It then passes a string to setInterval(), containing the following statement, which is set to execute once a second (every 1000 milliseconds):

```
ShowTime(O('time'))
```

Figure 19-2 shows this code (from *setinterval.htm* in the accompanying archive) running in a browser.

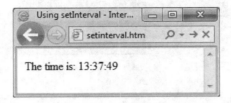

FIGURE 19-2 A simple clock created with **setInterval()**

Cancelling an Interval

To stop the repeating intervals previously set up from a call to setInterval(), you must previously have made a note of the interval's handle (also called the *interval ID*—not to be confused with an element ID), like this:

```
handle = setInterval("ShowTime(O('time'))", 1000)
```

Now you can stop the clock at any time by issuing the following call:

```
clearInterval(handle)
```

You can even set up a timer to stop the clock after a certain amount of time, like this:

```
setTimeout("clearInterval(handle)", 10000)
```

This statement will issue an interrupt in 10 seconds that will clear the repeating intervals. You can try this for yourself with the file *setinterval2.htm* in the accompanying archive.

A Simple Animation

By combining a few CSS properties with a repeating interrupt, you can produce all manner of animations and effects. For example, Figure 19-3 moves a square shape across the top of a browser, all the time ballooning up in size, before starting all over again.

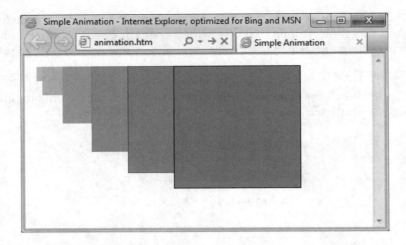

FIGURE 19-3 A simple animation (the current frame plus previous ones fading out)

The code used to produce the figure is as follows (and is saved as *animation.htm* in the accompanying archive):

```
<!DOCTYPE html>
<html>
  <head>
    <title>Simple Animation</title>
    <script src='mainfunctions.js'></script>
    <style>
      #box
      {
        position   :absolute;
        background:red;
        border     :1px solid black;
      }
    </style>
  </head>
  <body>
    <div id='box'></div>
    <script>
      SIZE = LEFT = 0

      setInterval(Animate, 30)

      function Animate()
      {
```

```
        SIZE += 10
        LEFT += 3

        if (SIZE == 200) SIZE = 0
        if (LEFT == 600) LEFT = 0

        S('box').width  = SIZE + 'px'
        S('box').height = SIZE + 'px'
        S('box').left   = LEFT + 'px'
      }
    </script>
  </body>
</html>
```

In the head of the document, the CSS ID of box is set to a background color of red with a 1-pixel black border, and its position is set to absolute so that it is allowed to be moved around in the browser.

Then in the Animate() function, the global variables SIZE and LEFT are continuously updated and then applied to the width, height, and left style attributes of the box object (adding px after each to specify that the values are in pixels), thus animating it at a frequency of once every 30 milliseconds.

 I'm sure you can think of some other attributes you could animate and will have fun playing with this example.

Web Workers

HTML5 web workers provide an even easier way for browsers to run multiple JavaScript threads in the background that can pass messages to each other, in much the same manner as the threads running in an operating system. You simply call up a new worker script that will sit there in the background either waiting for messages to be sent to it, which it will then act upon, or working away at something and sending messages only whenever it has any information to report.

This aims at achieving a significant speed increase over regular background JavaScripts, although getting to grips with programming them is likely to require a steep rather than gradual learning curve. Here's how to find out if a browser supports web workers:

```
<script>
  if (!!window.Worker)
      alert("Web workers supported")
  else alert("Web workers not supported")
</script>
```

This script simply alerts you as to whether or not web workers are supported by the browser you are using. Once you have determined that the browser will use them, you can run code such as the following, which calculates prime numbers in the background (saved as *webworkers.htm* in the accompanying archive):

```
<p>The highest prime number discovered so far is:
  <output id='result'></output></p>
<script>
  var worker = new Worker('worker.js')

  worker.onmessage = function(event)
  {
    O('result').innerHTML = event.data;
  }
</script>
```

This script displays some text and creates an element with the id of `result` into which the highest prime number found so far is continuously written. This is achieved by creating the new object called *worker* by calling the `Worker()` function, and passing it the name of an external JavaScript file called *worker.js* (explained shortly).

The `onmessage` event of the `worker` object is then attached to by the code. This triggers only when there is a new message to display, and the code that is called copies the data in `event.data` into the `innerHTML` property of the `result` element. After the code exits, it will not be called again until another message is ready to display.

The code that does the prime number calculation is saved separately in the *worker.js*, and looks like this:

```
var n = 1

search: while (true)
{
  n += 1

  for (var i = 2 ; i <= Math.sqrt(n) ; i += 1)
    if (n % i == 0) continue search

  postMessage(n)
}
```

This is a simple iterative piece of code that increases the value of n, starting from 1. After each increase, all values of 2 up to the square root of n are tested to see whether they are a factor of n. If any of them is, then n cannot be prime and so the `continue` keyword forces execution to go back to the start of the `search:` loop to see whether n + 1 is prime, and so on.

But if n is found to have no factors, it is prime and the `continue` keyword is not encountered, so program flow drops through to the `postMessage()` call, which posts the value n, creating an `onmessage` event on the `worker` object in the preceding code. The result of running this code is a line of text at the top of the browser that continuously updates and looks like this:

```
The highest prime number discovered so far is:  42737
```

Working together, an HTML page and associated JavaScript file can work away in the background, performing all manner of tasks, something that was achievable in the past only by manually creating events to run the code a few instructions at a time before returning to allow the web page to have some processor cycles, after which the event is then created to let the program code run a few more cycles, and so on.

As you might imagine, the old way is rather tricky and can be cumbersome. It can also mess with smooth animations on your web page if you don't get the event timings and time sharing exactly right. But with web workers, you can forget all about these things and simply place your background code into its own file, and just ensure the code calls the `postMessage()` function whenever it has something to say.

For full details on the web worker specifications, you can check out the official website at *tinyurl.com/webworkerspecs*.

Summary

This lesson has given you the tools you need to extend your web pages into powerful web applications, and to create seamless, behind-the-scenes programs to complete tasks without interrupting the smooth flow of the foreground process.

In the final lesson we'll take this one step further and round off your introduction to JavaScript by looking at how to implement background communication between a web server and web browser using Ajax.

Self-Test Questions

Using these questions, test how much you have learned in this lesson. If you don't know an answer, go back and reread the relevant section until your knowledge is complete. You can find the answers in Appendix A.

1. Which function do you call to set an interrupt to occur at a specific time in the future?

2. Which function do you call to set interrupts to occur at repeating intervals?

3. How can you cancel a timeout from occurring?

4. How can you cancel repeating interrupts from occurring?

5. What measurement of time is used for timeouts and intervals?

6. How can you test whether a browser supports web workers?

7. How do you create a new web worker?

8. What event is used by web workers to communicate with a calling process?

9. What function is used to send a message to a calling process?

10. Which property of the worker event contains the posted message?

Using Ajax

 To view the accompanying video for this lesson, please visit mhprofessional.com/nixonjavascript/.

Ajax is the power behind what came to be known as *Web 2.0*. It transformed the Internet because it replaced static pages that had to be posted using forms to make changes with much simpler behind-the-scenes communication with a web server, so that you merely had to type on a web page for that data to get sent to the server. Likewise, Ajax-enabled sites offer assistance whenever you need it, for example, by instantly telling you whether a username you desire is available before you submit your signup details.

The term *Ajax* actually stands for Asynchronous JavaScript and XML. However, nowadays it almost never uses XML because Ajax can communicate in so much more than that particular markup language. For example, it can transfer images and videos or other files.

Initially, writing Ajax code was considered a black art that only the most advanced programmers knew how to implement. But it's not actually the case. Ajax is relatively straightforward, as I'll show you now.

Creating an Ajax Object

The first thing you need to do in order to communicate with a web server via Ajax is to create a new object, as performed by the following function (some of which I showed you in Lesson 14, explaining the `try` and `catch()` keywords):

```
function CreateAjaxObject(callback)
{
  try
  {
    var ajax = new XMLHttpRequest()
```

```
  }
  catch(e1)
  {
    try
    {
      ajax = new ActiveXObject("Msxml2.XMLHTTP")
    }
    catch(e2)
    {
      try
      {
        ajax = new ActiveXObject("Microsoft.XMLHTTP")
      }
      catch(e3)
      {
        ajax = false
      }
    }
  }

  if (ajax) ajax.onreadystatechange = function()
  {
    if (this.readyState    == 4    &&
        this.status        == 200 &&
        this.responseText != null)
      callback.call(this.responseText)
  }
  else return false

  return ajax
}
```

Let's break this down, because it's quite long but actually easy to understand. To start with, the `CreateAjaxObject()` function accepts the argument `callback`, which I'll explain shortly, and then a sequence of `try` and `catch()` keywords attempts to use three different methods to create a new Ajax object in `ajax`.

The reason for this is that different versions of Microsoft's Internet Explorer browser use different methods for this, whereas all other browsers use yet another method. The upshot of the code is that if the browser supports Ajax (which all major modern browsers do), a new object called `ajax` is created.

In the second part of the function there's a pair of nested `if()` statements. The outer one is entered only if the `ajax` object was created; otherwise, `false` is returned to signal failure.

On success, an anonymous function is attached to the `onreadystatechange` event of the `ajax` object:

```
ajax.onreadystatechange = function()
```

This event is triggered whenever anything new happens in the Ajax exchange with the server. Therefore, by attaching to it, the code can listen in and be ready to receive any data sent to the browser by the server:

```
if (this.readyState    == 4    &&
    this.status        == 200 &&
    this.responseText != null)
  callback.call(this.responseText)
```

Here the attached function checks the `readyState` property of the `this` keyword (which represents the `ajax` object), and if it has a value of 4, the server has sent some data. If that's the case, then if `this.status` has a value of 200, and the data sent by the server is meaningful and not an error. Finally, if `this.responseText` doesn't have a value of `null`, the data was not just an empty string, so the `callback.call()` method is called:

```
callback.call(this.responseText)
```

I mentioned `callback` at the start of this explanation. It is the name of a function passed to the `CreateAjaxObject()` function, so that `CreateAjaxObject()` can call `callback()` when new Ajax data is received. The `callback()` function takes the value received in `this.responseText`, which is the data returned by the web server. I'll explain what goes into the `callback()` function a little later.

The `PostAjaxRequest()` Function

You will never have to call `CreateAjaxObject()` yourself because there are two more functions to complete the Ajax process (which will do the calling of `CreateAjaxObject()` for you): one for communicating with the server by Post requests and the other for using Get requests.

The `PostAjaxRequest()` function takes three arguments: the name of your callback function to receive data from the server, a URL with which to communicate with the server, and a string containing arguments to post to the server. It looks like this:

```
function PostAjaxRequest(callback, url, args)
{
  var contenttype = 'application/x-www-form-urlencoded'
  var ajax        = new CreateAjaxObject(callback)
  if (!ajax) return false

  ajax.open('POST', url, true)
  ajax.setRequestHeader('Content-type',    contenttype)
  ajax.setRequestHeader('Content-length', args.length)
  ajax.setRequestHeader('Connection',      'close')
  ajax.send(args)
  return true
}
```

What this function does is first set `contenttype` to a string value that enables encoded form data to be transmitted:

```
var contenttype = 'application/x-www-form-urlencoded'
```

Then either the new `ajax` object is created or `false` is returned to indicate an error was encountered:

```
var ajax = new CreateAjaxObject(callback)
if (!ajax) return false
```

Now that an `ajax` object has been created, the following lines open the Ajax request with a call to the `open()` method of the `ajax` object and send headers to the server via a Post request, including the `contenttype` string, the length of the `args` argument, and a header ready to close the connection:

```
ajax.open('POST', url, true)
ajax.setRequestHeader('Content-type',   contenttype)
ajax.setRequestHeader('Content-length', args.length)
ajax.setRequestHeader('Connection',     'close')
```

The data is then sent, the connection is closed, and a value of `true` returned to indicate success:

```
ajax.send(args)
return true
```

The `GetAjaxRequest()` Function

The `PostAjaxRequest()` function comes with a sister function that performs exactly the same process, but it sends the data using a Get request. You need to have both functions in your toolkit because some servers you may interact with require Post requests, and some will need Get requests for their Ajax calls.

Here's what the partner `GetAjaxRequest()` function looks like:

```
function GetAjaxRequest(callback, url, args)
{
  var nocache = '&nocache=' + Math.random() * 1000000
  var ajax = new CreateAjaxObject(callback)
  if (!ajax) return false

  ajax.open('GET', url + '?' + args + nocache, true)
  ajax.send(null)
  return true
}
```

One of the main differences between this and the `PostAjaxRequest()` function is that a variable called `nocache` is created from a random number so that a unique value can be added to the query string sent by each Get request, which will prevent any caching the server, browser, or a proxy server might perform by ensuring every request sent is unique:

```
var nocache = '&nocache=' + Math.random() * 1000000
```

The next couple of lines are the same as the `PostAjaxRequest()` function. They create a new `ajax` object, or return `false` if that fails:

```
var ajax = new CreateAjaxObject(callback)
if (!ajax) return false
```

Finally, the Get request is made with a call to the `open()` method of the `ajax` object, the request is sent, and then `true` is returned to indicate success:

```
ajax.open('GET', url + '?' + args + nocache, true)
ajax.send(null)
return true
```

The `callback()` Function

Now we are ready to create our `callback()` function that will receive the data sent back to JavaScript via Ajax. This is another instance where the `this` keyword must be used, as follows:

```
function callback()
{
  O('mydiv').innerHTML = this
}
```

This code assumes that the `O()` function has been included in the page, and it supplies the value passed to the function in `this` to the `innerHTML` property of a `<div>` with the `id` of `mydiv`. All that remains to do is create the `<div>`, like this:

```
<div id='mydiv'></div>
```

And now we are ready to call either the `PostAjaxRequest()` or the `GetAjaxRequest()` function, like this:

```
PostAjaxRequest(callback, 'ajax.php', 'url=http://yahoo.com')
```

Or, like this:

```
GetAjaxRequest(callback, 'ajax.php', 'url=http://yahoo.com')
```

In either instance, a program in the same folder as the calling code, called `ajax.php`, is chosen for the communication, and the URL *http://yahoo.com* is sent to the program as the value of the key `url`.

The `ajax.htm` Example

Here's a document that uses Ajax in just the manner described in the previous section. It is saved as *ajax.htm* in the accompanying archive:

```html
<!DOCTYPE html>
<html>
  <head>
    <title>Using Ajax</title>
    <script src='mainfunctions.js'></script>
    <script src='ajaxfunctions.js'></script>
    <style>
      body {
        background:#ddd;
      }
      #head {
        font-size   :16pt;
        font-family:sans-serif;
      }
      #mydiv {
        border:5px solid black;
        margin:25px;
      }
    </style>
  </head>
  <body>
    <p id='head'>The Yahoo! homepage will appear in the div below:</p>

    <div id='mydiv'>Loading...</div>

    <script>
      PostAjaxRequest(callback, 'ajax.php', 'url=http://yahoo.com')

      function callback()
      {
        O('mydiv').innerHTML = this
      }
    </script>
  </body>
</html>
```

The CSS used in the `<head>` section is not strictly necessary, but it helps lay out the page a little more clearly. The important parts to note are the `<div>` with the ID of `mydiv` and the `<script>` section, in which the `PostAjaxRequest()` function is called, and the `callback()` function where the `innerHTML` property of the `<div>` is written to with the data returned by the Ajax call.

The `ajax.php` Program

The last part of the Ajax puzzle is to write the program that will reside on the web server and communicate with the web browser. Server programs can be written in many different languages, including PHP, Perl, and C. But PHP is the easiest and most commonly implemented language, especially for quick tasks—in this case, the PHP code is a pair of two instructions that look like this:

```php
<?php
  if     (isset($_GET['url']))  echo file_get_contents($_GET['url']);
  elseif (isset($_POST['url'])) echo file_get_contents($_POST['url']);
?>
```

The syntax of this code is very similar to JavaScript, so it's easy to follow. What it does is test whether the key `url` has been sent to it, either in a Get request (as `$_GET['url']`) or in a Post request (as `$_POST['url']`).

In either case, the PHP `file_get_contents()` function is called on the value passed to it (which in this case is *http://yahoo.com*). This fetches the web page referred to, which is then returned to the calling Ajax function using the PHP `echo` keyword (which is like JavaScript's `document.write()`).

Figure 20-1 shows the result of running the previous Ajax example, which then communicates with *ajax.php* (also in the archive) on the web server, to insert the contents of the *Yahoo!* home page into a `<div>` element.

FIGURE 20-1   The Yahoo! home page has been pulled into a **`<div>`** via Ajax.

You may notice that in Figure 20-1 some of the Yahoo! home page has located itself above the `<div>`, and the #ddd background color the CSS had applied to the web page has been overwritten. This is because elements are being moved to absolute locations and other properties are being changed by the CSS rules applied to the page—there are, it turns out, a number of conflicts. But there is a solution to this.

The `ajax2.htm` Example

Although it dramatically illustrates the power of Ajax, loading an entire document into a `<div>` element is not a good idea because that document will have its own `<html>`, `<head>`, `<body>`, and other duplicated sections that could conflict with the main document. However, I wanted to illustrate accessing the `innerHTML` property of an element for the purposes of displaying information obtained from an Ajax call.

But a better way to load an entire document (other than attaching its URL to the `src` attribute) might be to insert the result of the Ajax call into an `<iframe>` element, because it is suitable for containing a stand-alone document such that it won't conflict with the parent.

Here's an example illustrating how you would do this. It is saved as *ajax2.htm* in the accompanying archive and is simply a reworking of the *ajax.htm* document:

```
<!DOCTYPE html>
<html>
  <head>
    <title>Using Ajax</title>
    <script src='mainfunctions.js'></script>
    <script src='ajaxfunctions.js'></script>
    <style>
      body {
        background:#ddd;
      }
      #iframe {
        border:5px solid black;
        margin:10px 25px;
      }
    </style>
  </head>
  <body>
    <h2>The Yahoo! homepage will appear in the iframe below:</h2>

    <iframe id='iframe' width='96%' height='1000'></iframe>

    <script>
      PostAjaxRequest(callback, 'ajax.php', 'url=http://yahoo.com')
```

```
    function callback()
    {
      O('iframe').contentWindow.document.write(this)
    }
  </script>
 </body>
</html>
```

In this version, the CSS is a little different and the `<div>` is replaced with an `<iframe>` element, as shown in Figure 20-2. To cater for this, the `callback()` function now uses the `document.write()` function to write the data returned by the Ajax call into the `<iframe>` (instead of the previous code that wrote into the `innerHTML` property of a `<div>`). It does this by writing into the `contentWindow` object of the `<iframe>` like this:

```
O('iframe').contentWindow.document.write(this)
```

FIGURE 20-2   The Yahoo! home page has been pulled into an `<iframe>` via Ajax.

Therefore, those are two different methods you can use for outputting the data returned from an Ajax call. Others include changing the `value` property of `<input>` elements, the `src` property of `<img>` elements, or simply the `style` properties of any element, according to how you wish to interpret, display, or otherwise deal with the information received via Ajax.

Ajax Security Restrictions

To prevent cross-browser attacks, the way Ajax is implemented is very secure. Only the server issuing a web page containing Ajax code can communicate with that page. This prevents third-party servers muscling in and trying to steal your private data, or injecting unwanted advertisements, and so on. Also, local file systems do not work with Ajax.

Therefore, if you wish to experiment with developing Ajax code, you need a web server (either local or remote) and must store your test files there, calling them up in your browser via an *http://* prefix in its address bar.

Because you may not be able to test this code on your own computer if you don't have a web server, I have uploaded *ajax.htm*, *ajax2.htm*, and *ajax.php* (along with the supporting JavaScript files) to this book's companion website. You can therefore try out the examples in this section by visiting *20lessons.com/ajax.htm* and *20lessons.com/ajax2.htm*.

For ease of access, I have saved the three Ajax functions in the file *ajaxfunctions.js* in the accompanying archive so that you can include them in the `<head>` of a web page that will use Ajax communication, like this:

```
<script src='ajaxfunctions.js'></script>
```

The `OnDOMReady()` Function

I'd like to leave you with one final function to help your JavaScript run as fast as possible, the `OnDOMReady()` function. If you have a web page in which you want the JavaScript to run as soon as all the HTML is parsed and the DOM is ready (but before all resources like images are loaded and ready), then you can wrap your main section of JavaScript in the following:

```
OnDOMReady(function()
{
  // Place all your
  // JavaScript statements
  // in this section
})

// Your functions
// can go here
```

All you need to do now is ensure that the following function is alongside your code so that it can trigger your main JavaScript at the earliest possible time that the DOM is complete and ready to be accessed:

```
function OnDOMReady(func)
{
  var timer = setInterval(onChange, 5)
  var ready = false

  if(document.addEventListener)
    document.addEventListener(
  "DOMContentLoaded", onChange, false)

document.onreadystatechange = window.onload = onChange

function onChange(e)
  {
    if(e && e.type == "DOMContentLoaded")
    {
      fireDOMReady()
    }
    else if(e && e.type == "load")
    {
      fireDOMReady()
    }
    else if(document.readyState)
    {
      if((/loaded|complete/).test(document.readyState))
      {
        fireDOMReady()
      }
      else if(!!document.documentElement.doScroll)
      {
        try
        {
          ready || document.documentElement.doScroll('left')
        }
        catch(e)
        {
          return
        }
```

```
                fireDOMReady()
            }
        }
    }
}

function fireDOMReady()
{
  if(!ready)
  {
    ready = true
    func.call()

    if(document.removeEventListener)
       document.removeEventListener(
      "DOMContentLoaded", onChange, false)

    clearInterval(timer) document.onreadystatechange =
      window.onload = timer = null
  }
 }
}
```

This code is quite complex, so I won't explain how it works. But I have saved the function in the accompanying archive in the file *ondomloaded.js* so that you can include it in the <head> of any web page that requires the fastest possible initiation, like this:

```
<script src='ondomready.js'></script>
```

Summary

And that, as they say, is that! You've reached the end of this book, and I hope you found it as easy to follow as I promised at the start. You now have all the skills you need to be a proficient JavaScript programmer and are well on your way to creating popular and dynamic websites. Before you go, though, take a browse through the appendix of JavaScript functions. I've listed most of them (omitting more obscure or technical functions) so that you'll have a handy reference to quickly see how to implement the features you need.

Thanks for reading this book. I hope you've learned everything you set out to learn and, if you feel so inclined, will be very grateful if you would take a moment to leave a review of this book on your favorite book retailing website. Good luck with your web development!

Self-Test Questions

Using these questions, test how much you have learned in this lesson. If you don't know an answer, go back and reread the relevant section until your knowledge is complete. You can find the answers in Appendix A.

1. Which keyword and function is used to let JavaScript try out the three methods of creating an Ajax object in turn?

2. Which event of an Ajax object informs JavaScript whenever its ready state changes?

3. What property of the `onreadystatechange` event contains the ready state?

4. What property of the `onreadystatechange` event contains the status of the Ajax call?

5. What property of the `onreadystatechange` event contains the response text from the Ajax call?

6. What is the purpose of a callback function?

7. How do you call a callback function?

8. What is the reason for adding a random string to Ajax Get requests?

9. Which property is used to overwrite the HTML content of an element?

10. Why is the supplied `OnDOMReady()` function superior to using the built-in `onload()` function?

PART III

Appendixes

Answers to the Self-Test Questions

This appendix contains the answers to all the questions posed at the end of the lessons in this book. To ensure you have understood everything, try to refrain from checking these answers until you have attempted to answer all the questions in a lesson.

If you don't know an answer, try to find it in the book before you look here if you can, as this will help you remember it next time.

Lesson 1 Answers

1. ECMAScript is the name of the official language of which JavaScript and Jscript are dialects.

2. JavaScript is so named due to a marketing tie-in with the Java programming language name; JavaScript is actually not very similar to Java.

3. The trademark for the name JavaScript is owned by Oracle Corporation due to its purchase of Sun Microsystems, which developed Java.

4. It was necessary to create a new programming language (rather than simply embed an existing one such as C) in order to support tight integration with (and manipulation of) HTML elements.

5. HTML stands for HyperText Markup Language—this is the language used to separate HTML documents into their various elements and to describe the basic form and content of a web page.

6. HTTP stands for HyperText Transfer Protocol—this is the method used for communicating between a web browser and server to transfer HTML (and other) documents.

7. CSS stands for Cascading Style Sheets—a system for styling HTML elements without altering a document's contents.

205

8. DOM stands for Document Object Model—the system devised for separating all parts of an HTML document into separate elements, or objects.

9. JavaScript's Math and Date objects are based on those of the Java language— this is about as close as the two languages get.

10. To view the source of a web page in all major browsers, right-click the document and then select View Source or View Page Source. In some browsers, a new window will open, while others may display the source in a tab.

Lesson 2 Answers

1. To create a single-line comment, start it with the sequence //. For a multiline comment, start it with the sequence /* and end with */.

2. You do not need to end lines of code with a semicolon unless you intend to include another instruction on the same line, in which case the semicolon will act as a new line to separate them. However, if you begin a new line with either a left parenthesis or left bracket (either (or [), you should place a semicolon either at the start of that line or at the end of the preceding one; otherwise, JavaScript will run the two lines together.

3. JavaScript can be included in the <head> of a document or the <body>, or it can be saved in an external file and loaded in where needed, using the src attribute of the <script> tag.

4. JavaScript is case sensitive; the variables YourName, yourname, and YOURNAME are all different and contain separate values.

5. Variable names must begin with either an upper- (A-Z) or lowercase (a-z) letter, or the $ or _ symbols, and may include any of these characters afterward, as well as the digits 0-9.

6. To add values together, use the + operator, for example, result = 23 + 7.

7. To concatenate a string, use the + operator, for example, greeting = "Hello " + YourName. JavaScript works out that the + is being used for string concatenation rather than addition.

8. To incorporate a quotation mark within a string that is enclosed with the same character, escape it with a \ character, for example: "He said, \"Hello\".".

9. To change a string to a number, you can pass it to the Number() function, for example, result = Number("12345").

10. In JavaScript, NaN stands for Not a Number, a result you may encounter when a failed attempt is made to convert a value to a number.

Lesson 3 Answers

1. The ++ operator increments a variable by 1 (inversely, -- decrements by 1).

2. The + + operator can be used in either pre- or post-incrementing mode. The expression if (++a) uses pre-incrementing; it increments a and then performs the if evaluation. On the other hand, the expression if (a++) is evaluated using the current value in a, and only then is it post-incremented.

3. The % operator is used to calculate the modulus of a division operation (the part left over, or the remainder), for example, 20 % 7 returns a modulus of 6 because 7 goes into 20 twice (making 14), leaving a remainder of 6.

4. To assign a value to a variable, you use the = operator, for example, area = Math.PI * radius * radius (Math.PI being a constant containing the value π).

5. To increment a variable by a specified value, use the += operator, for example, a += 27.

6. To turn a value from negative to positive, use the Math.abs() function, for example, Math.abs(myvar). If myvar is negative (such as −92), the value returned is positive (for example, 92); if it is zero or positive, the value returned is simply myvar.

7. To create a random number with a value between 1 and 60 inclusive, call the Math.random() function and turn its result into an integer with Math.floor(), like this: Math.floor(Math.random() * 60) + 1. The + 1 is required at the end because the preceding expression returns a random number between 0 and 59.

8. There are three functions that turn floating point numbers into integers: Math .floor() rounds down to the next lowest integer, Math.ceil() rounds up to the next highest integer, and Math.round() rounds down or up to whichever is the nearest integer value.

9. In JavaScript, the addition operator is also used to concatenate strings, for example, happy_singer = 'Pharrell' + ' ' + 'Williams'.

10. The expression a = a / 20 can be written more succinctly as a /= 20.

Lesson 4 Answers

1. To check whether two values are equal, you use the == operator, for example, if (score == 21).

2. The == operator tests for two expressions having the same value, whereas the === operator is the same, but tests whether they are also of the same type. For example, 23 == '23' is true because both sides evaluate to the number 23, but 23 === '23' is false because the former is a number but the latter is a string.

3. The values returned by JavaScript to indicate whether an expression evaluates or not are `true` for success or `false` for failure.

4. To test whether two expressions both evaluate to `true`, use the `&&` operator, for example, `if (score == 21 && level == 3)`.

5. To test whether at least one of two expressions is `true`, use the `||` operator, for example, `if (city == 'Dallas' || state == 'Texas')`.

6. To test whether an expression is not true, use the `!` operator, for example, `if (!(input == 'quit'))`.

7. The `*` operator has a higher precedence than `+` because multiplication and division occur before addition and subtraction.

8. The operator with the lowest precedence is the `,` (comma) operator, which is used to separate expressions or arguments.

9. The `*`, `/`, `+`, and `-` operators all evaluate from left to right (except where overridden by operator precedence).

10. You can shorten code that refers to an object by using a `with` statement, for example, `with (string) { alert(length) }`. Care must be taken when using this statement as its use can be ambiguous (i.e., to which element does the length property refer?) potentially leading to obscure bugs.

Lesson 5 Answers

1. The first character of an array name must be either an upper- (A–Z) or lowercase (a–z) letter, or the `$` or `_` character.

2. After the first character, an array name may include any of the characters that can begin an array or variable name, and any of the digits 0–9.

3. To create a new array called `mydata`, use code such as `mydata = new Array()`.

4. To specify an array's initial length, you can supply a single value within the parentheses representing the length, like this: `mydata = new Array(20)`.

5. To reference item 11 (the element at index 11) in the array `mydata`, refer to it like this: `mydata[11]`.

6. The first item in an array is always at index 0.

7. You may populate an array with data when you create it by providing a list of values, like this: `mydata = new Array('peas', 'corn', 'nuts')`. Beware if you supply only a single numeric value, as this will instead set the initial length of the array to that value.

8. An associative array is one in which its elements are accessed in key/value pairs rather than numeric indexes.

9. To add the key/value pair of Name / Alice as a new element in the associative array mydata, use code such as this: mydata['Name'] = 'Alice', or create the array like this: mydata = { 'Name' : 'Alice' }.

10. To retrieve the value for the key Name in the associative array mydata, use code such as this: variable = mydata['Name'].

Lesson 6 Answers

1. To create a multidimensional array, you place additional arrays within elements of a parent array.

2. To access a two-dimensional numeric array, follow the array name with two pairs of square brackets, with numeric index values in each, for example, myarray[23][17].

3. To access a two-dimensional associative array, follow the array name with two pairs of square brackets, with key values in each, for example, myarray['cheese']['mature'].

4. You may nest as many levels of arrays as there is room for in memory. There is no hard and fast rule, but each deeper level requires an order of magnitude more memory. For example, a 10×10 array would use 100 memory locations, $10 \times 10 \times 10$ would use 1000, and $10 \times 10 \times 10 \times 10$ would use 10,000, and so on.

5. One way to construct a multidimensional array for a class of 30 history students to hold their grades for a year's two semesters would be to create a master array populated with sub-arrays for the semesters, for example, students[0-29][0-1] for 0–29 students, with 0–1 semesters each.

6. To extend this array to handle four years' worth of semesters, you could add a third level between that of the students and the semesters to represent the years, like this: students[0-29][0-3][0-1] for 0–29 students, with 0–3 years each, within which there are 0–1 semesters for each.

7. In the chessboard example, code to represent the black player responding by moving *pawn to queen 4* might be Board[1][3] = '-'; Board[3][3] = 'p'.

8. Code to represent the white player's pawn at king 4 taking the black player's pawn might be Board[4][4] = '-'; Board[3][3] = 'P'.

9. To turn a three-dimensional chessboard array into a four-dimensional array, you would need to add a further level after the third level, like this: 1 master array → 8 sub-arrays → 64 sub–sub-arrays → 512 sub–sub-sub-arrays.

10. To increment the stock of toddlers' bricks by 12, you could use code such as this: Categories['Toddlers']['Wooden Bricks']['Stock'] += 12.

Lesson 7 Answers

1. To iterate through an array one element at a time with `for (… in …)`, use it like this: `for (i in myarray) document.write(myarray[i])`.

2. The `forEach()` function is similar to using `for (… in …)` to iterate through an array, but is simpler to implement. For example, you could use this to iterate through `myarray`: `myarray.forEach(myfunc);` however, you must have already written the function `myfunc` to process the array.

3. You can join two arrays together with the `concat()` function, for example, `programs = utilities.concat(applications)`.

4. To join together two arrays called `tennis` and `golf` into a third called `sports`, you could use either `sports = tennis.concat(golf)` or `sports = golf .concat(tennis)`.

5. To quickly pass an entire array to a function, simply pass the array name without the `[]` brackets, for example, `document.write(sports)`. Here, the resulting output is a comma-separated string.

6. To invoke a function on each element of an array, you could use the `map()` function; for example, `integers = floats.map(Math.round)` applies the `Math.round` function (which converts floating point values to integers) to every element in the array `floats` (a set of floating point numbers). The resulting values are then saved in the array `integers`.

7. Contrary to what you might assume, the `join()` function doesn't join arrays together (that is achieved with the `concat()` function); instead, it joins all elements of an array together into a single string.

8. To display all the elements in the array `sports` as a string, with each separated from the next by the string `' plus '`, you would use the `join()` function, for example, `document.write(sports.join(' plus '))`.

9. The command `document.write(hobbies)` displays all the elements in the array `hobbies`, separated by commas.

10. The command `activities = sports.concat(hobbies)` creates the new array `activities`, populating it with all the elements from the `sports` and `hobbies` arrays.

Lesson 8 Answers

1. The `push()` function adds a new element to the bottom of an array, for example, `myarray.push(value)`.

2. The `pop()` function removes an element from the bottom of an array, for example, `value = myarray.pop()`.

3. The `unshift()` function adds a new element to the top of an array, for example, `myarray.unshift(value)`.

4. The `shift()` function removes an element from the top of an array, for example, `value = myarray.shift()`.

5. A First In/Last Out (FILO) array is also known as a *stack*.

6. A First In/First Out (FIFO) array is also known as a *buffer*.

7. You invert the order of elements in an array using the `reverse()` function; for example, `myarray.reverse()` will reverse the array in place.

8. You can determine the number of elements in an array by accessing its `length` property, for example, `count = myarray.length`.

9. The name given to the process of a section of code repeatedly calling itself is recursion. A common programmer's joke goes, "Question: *What is the dictionary definition for recursion? Answer: See recursion!*".

10. A stack structure (being FILO) is best suited for recursive programming, as described in Question 9.

Lesson 9 Answers

1. To sort an array alphabetically in ascending order, call the `sort()` function on it, for example, `myarray.sort()`.

2. To sort an array alphabetically in descending order, call the `sort()` and `reverse()` functions on it, for example, `myarray.sort().reverse()`.

3. To sort an array numerically in ascending order, create an external function that returns the first argument minus the second one, like this: `function SortNumeric(a, b) { return a - b }`. Then call that function in the `sort()` function, for example, `myarray.sort(SortNumeric)`.

4. To sort an array numerically in descending order, create an external function that returns the second argument minus the first one, like this: `function SortDescend(a, b) { return b - a }`. Then call that function in the `sort()` function, for example, `myarray.sort(SortDescend)`. Or you can perform an ascending numeric search and use the `reverse()` function.

5. To sort an array numerically in ascending order with an inline function, use code such as `myarray.sort(function(a, b) { return a - b })`.

6. To sort an array numerically in descending order with an inline function, use code such as `myarray.sort(function(a, b) { return b - a })`.

7. You can insert and remove elements from an array in the same command by using the `splice()` function.

8. The command `fruits.splice(4, 2)` removes two elements from the array `fruits` starting at index 4 (the fifth element—*another great movie*).

9. The command `fruits.splice(5, 0, 'Apples', 'Pears')` inserts the values `Apples` and `Pears` at index location 5 (the sixth element—*will that be the sequel?*) in the array `fruits`.

10. By issuing the command `fruits.splice(6, 2, 'Apples', 'Pears', 'Grapes')`, two elements are removed from the array `fruits` at index 6 (the seventh element—*which... oh, never mind!*), and then replaced with the values `Apples`, `Pears`, and `Grapes`.

Lesson 10 Answers

1. You can have JavaScript do something if an expression is true using the `if()` statement, for example, `if (score > high_score) { ... }`.

2. In an `if()` statement, you do not need braces unless there would be more than one statement within them.

3. To provide a second option to an `if()` statement for when an expression is `false`, use the `else` statement, for example, `if (this == that) { ... } else { ... }`.

4. You can extend `if()` statements to make further tests by placing another `if()` statement following an `else`, for example, `if (this == that) { ... } else if { ... }`.

5. The best statement to use when you wish to test an expression or variable for a range of values and act differently on each is the `switch()` statement, for example, `switch(result) { ... }`.

6. To test a value in a `switch()` statement, use the `case` keyword, for example, `case 42`.

7. After the value following a `case` keyword, you must place a colon before the instructions to execute, for example, `case 42: dothis()`.

8. In a `switch()` statement, the `default` keyword processes all remaining values not specifically handled.

9. In a `switch()` statement, the `break` keyword is used to jump out of the `switch()` to the following statement.

10. Braces are not required to enclose the instructions for each case of a `switch()` statement (but may be used if desired). The statements are listed following the colon after a `case` keyword and are normally (but not always) terminated with a `break` keyword.

Lesson 11 Answers

1. The condition of a `while()` loop is tested before each iteration.

2. The condition of a `do ... while()` loop is tested after each iteration.

3. It is preferable to use `do ... while()` in place of `while()` when at least one iteration of a loop is needed.

4. One way to display the 8 times table with a `while()` loop would be: `j = 1; while (j <= 12) document.write(j + ' times 8 = ' + j++ * 8 + '<br>')`.

5. A `for()` loop requires three arguments (or sets of arguments): one or more initializers, a test statement, and one or more statements to run after each iteration.

6. To include additional initialization statements in a `for()` loop, separate them with commas.

7. To include additional statements to the third argument of a `for()` loop, separate them with commas.

8. A `for(... in ...)` loop iterates through an array one item at a time, for example, `for (element in myarray) { ... }`.

9. To break out of a loop, use a `break` statement.

10. To skip the current iteration of a loop and move on to the next one, use a `continue` statement.

Lesson 12 Answers

1. The main purpose of a function is to combine a sequence of one or more instructions into a single unit that can be called by name and that (optionally) can be passed and/or can return values.

2. An anonymous function is one that has not been given a name and that is attached directly to the code that references it.

3. Being in line with code, you should avoid using anonymous functions when you find you need to use the same function in more than one place. In which case, rather than creating redundant extra instances, it's better to make each a named function and simply refer to the single function by name wherever it is called.

4. The main way a value is returned by a function is via the use of a `return` keyword.

5. To pass values to a function, place them in the parentheses following the function name, separated with commas, for example, `myfunc(arg1, arg2, arg3)`.

6. To access the values passed to a function, its declaration should list a series of variable names in parentheses, each of which will have the value associated with its position assigned to it.

7. You can also access the arguments passed to a function using its `arguments` object, for example, `for (i in arguments) document.write( arguments[i])`.

8. When you wish a function to accept an unknown number of different arguments, it is best to use the `arguments` object rather than named arguments.

9. When a function is called by attaching it to an object using a period (for example, `myarray.join()`), the function is passed to an object called `this` that refers to the attached object (in this instance, `myarray`).

10. To tell a function that a variable is to be used only locally, the first time it is referenced, you can preface it with a `var` keyword, for example, `for (var j = 0 ; j < 10 ; ++j) { ... }`. Variables not prefaced in this manner are treated as having global scope.

Lesson 13 Answers

1. To declare a class, you use the same syntax as for a function.

2. To create a new instance of a class, you use the `new` keyword, for example, `User = new userclass(fname, lname)`. Or, if no arguments are required to be passed, simply `User = new userclass()`.

3. To declare properties in a class declaration, attach them to the `this` keyword, for example, `this.firstname = fname`.

4. To declare methods in a class declaration, either attach an anonymous or a named function to the `this` keyword and method name, for example, `this.getName = function() { ... }`. Or, if you already have a named function (called, for example, `myfunc`), you can attach it like this: `this.getName = myfunc`.

5. Once you have an object created from a class using the `new` keyword, you can access its properties by name, for example, `User.firstname = 'Alice'`, or `document.write(User.firstname)`.

6. Once you have an object created from a class using the `new` keyword, you can access its methods by name, for example, `document.write(User.getName())`.

7. The `prototype` keyword reduces memory usage by allowing reference to a single property or method when a new object is created. Rather than copying a property or method and embedding a copy of it in each new object created, only the single instance of that property or method will be used.

8. A static property or method is one of which there is only a single instance accessible from any object created from a class.

9. The `prototype` keyword is attached to the class name, and then the property or method that is being prototyped is attached to that, for example, `UserClass.prototype.getName = function() { ... }`, or `UserClass. prototype.appName = 'My App'`. These are static methods and properties.

10. You can add new functions to extend JavaScript by applying the `prototype` keyword to an existing class (such as `Array` or `String`), for example, `String.prototype.Repeat = function(r) { return new Array(++r).join(this) }`.

Lesson 14 Answers

1. You can trap JavaScript errors using the `onerror` event.

2. To trap errors in a whole document, attach the `onerror` event to the window object, or attach it to any individual element to trap errors only in that element, for example, `window.onerror = function(msg, url, line) { ... }` or `element.onerror = fixError`.

3. You can mark a section of code to be tried by a browser without it issuing errors by placing it in a `try` statement, for example, `try { ... }`. A `catch()` function or `finally` section must always be supplied with each `try` statement.

4. To handle an error caught using a `try` statement, use a matching `catch()` function, for example, `try { ... } catch(e) { ... }`.

5. A regular expression is a sequence of characters that forms a pattern for making searches and/or replacements.

6. You start and end a regular expression in JavaScript with the / character, for example, `/<.+>/`.

7. You can (a) check an object using a regular expression with the `test()` function (for example, `document.write(/sat/.test('The cat sat... '))`), and (b) modify an object with a regular expression using the `replace()` function (for example, `document.write('The cat sat... '.replace(/cat/, 'dog'))`).

8. To represent a whitespace character in a regular expression, use the `\s` metacharacter.

9. A shorter way to express the set of characters `abcdefghijk` in a regular expression is `a-k`.

10. To ensure an expression is applied both case insensitively and globally, place the `i` and `g` characters immediately following the expression, for example, `document.write('The cat sat... '.replace(/cat/ig, 'dog'))`.

Lesson 15 Answers

1. To return an object for an element based on its ID, call the `getElementById()` function, for example, `MyObject = document.getElementById('MyDiv')`.

2. To modify a style property of an object, access it like this: `obj.style.background = 'yellow'`.

3. To return an array of objects for all elements of a specified type in a document, call the `getElementsByTagName()` function, for example, `images = document.getElementsByTagName('img')`.

4. To set the font size of the object `MyObject` to 12 point using the `setAttribute()` function, use code such as `MyObject.setAttribute('style','font-size:12pt')`.

5. To set the font size of the object `MyObject` to 12 point without using the `setAttribute()` function, use code such as `MyObject.style.fontSize = '12pt'`.

6. To determine how much space there is available in the current window of the web browser, check the `innerHeight` and `innerWidth` properties of the window object, for example, `w = window.innerWidth; h = window.innerHeight`.

7. To determine the width and height of the screen of the user's device, check the `availWidth` and `availHeight` properties of the `screen` object, for example, `w = screen.availWidth; h = screen.availHeight`.

8. To change the title of the current document from JavaScript, access the `title` property of `document`, for example, `document.title = 'New title'`.

9. You can change the image displayed by an `<img>` tag by changing its `src` property, for example, `image.src = 'newimage.jpg'`.

10. You can change the width and height of an image (or other element) with the `width` and `height` properties of its `style` object, for example, `image.style.width = '100px'; image.style.height = '60px'`.

Lesson 16 Answers

1. To change the file displayed by an `<img>` tag to *newimage.jpg* when the mouse passes over it, change its `src` attribute value, for example, `<img src='photo.jpg' onmouseover="this.src='newimage.jpg'">`.

2. When an element is clicked, its `onclick` event is triggered. You could attach to it in the following manner: `onclick="this.src='newimage.jpg'"`.

3. You can create a new element using the `createElement()` function, passing it the type of element to create, for example, `newspan = document.createElement('span')`.

4. You can attach a new element to the DOM using the `appendChild()` function, for example, `document.body.appendChild(newspan)`.

5. You can remove an element from the DOM by calling the `removeChild()` function on the `parentNode` object of the element, for example, `element.parentNode.removeChild(element)`.

6. You can change the visibility of an object by manipulating its `visibility` property, supplying values of `hidden` or `visible`, for example, `MyObject.style.visibility = 'hidden'`.

7. To prevent an object from displaying at all, you can change its `display` property, for example, `MyObject.style.display = 'none'`.

8. You can stop and restart playback of HTML5 audio or video using the `play()` and `pause()` functions.

9. The `play()` and `pause()` functions should be attached to the `<audio>` or `<video>` element to which they apply.

10. You can specify whether or not the default play and other buttons display on an audio or video player by omitting or including the `controls` attribute, for example, `<audio controls>`.

Lesson 17 Answers

1. The `cookie` property of the current document holds its cookies in one long string; for example, `alert(document.cookie)` will display all the current cookies and their values.

2. To create a new cookie, assign it to `document.cookie`, for example, `document.cookie = 'cookiename=' + cookievalue`. Either a new cookie will be added or an existing one will be updated.

3. To read a cookie's value, you must process the `document.cookie` property string, searching for the cookie's name. When found, the value following the = sign is the cookie's value (in escaped format) and is terminated with a semicolon. The `substring()` function is a good way of pulling out just that part of the string.

4. To delete a cookie, you do the same as creating a cookie but provide an expiry time in the past, for example, `document.cookie = 'name=; expires=Thu, 01 Jan 1970 00:00:01 GMT'`. No value is supplied following the = because the cookie is to be deleted, and passing a value would be pointless.

5. The `domain` argument lets you limit the scope of a cookie to only a part of your website such as *blog.mydomain.com*.

6. To test whether a browser supports local storage, use an `if()` statement to check whether the `localStorage` object is not undefined, for example, `if (typeof localStorage != 'undefined') { /* Supported */ }`.

7. To save an item of data to local storage, call the `setItem()` function, for example, `localStorage.setItem('username', 'Mary')`.

8. To read an item of data from local storage, call the `getItem()` function, for example, `username = localStorage.getItem('username')`.

9. To remove an item of data from local storage, call the `removeItem()` function, for example, `localStorage.removeItem('username')`.

10. To empty all local storage for the current domain, call the `clear()` function, for example, `localStorage.clear()`.

Lesson 18 Answers

1. The best way to test whether a browser is Internet Explorer is to check whether the `document.all` object exists, for example, `if (document.all) agent = 'IE'`. If not, then check to see whether the substring `Trident` exists in the user agent string.

2. The best way to test whether a browser is Opera is to check whether the `window.opera` object exists, for example, `if (window.opera) agent = 'Opera'`. If not, then check to see whether the substring `OPR` exists in the user agent string.

3. You can test for all other browser types by interrogating the `userAgent` property of the `navigator` object, for example, `if (navigator.userAgent.indexOf('Chrome') != -1) agent = 'Chrome'`.

4. A query string is the tail part of a URL that contains data to be passed to a web page.

5. The character that immediately precedes a query string is the question mark (?).

6. The character that separates key/value pairs in a query string is the ampersand (&).

7. Space characters are represented by + signs in query strings (or by %20).

8. The `search` property of the `location` object of the current `window` contains the current query string, for example, `query = window.location.search.substr(1)`. The `substr()` in this example skips over the initial ? character that precedes the query string.

9. You can split key=value substrings from a query string into an array using the `split()` function with the & separator, for example, `parts = window .location.search.substr(1).split('&')`.

10. Given an array of key=value substrings called `parts`, you can turn each string element into a sub-array containing the key in its first element and value in its second using the `split()` function with the = separator, like this: `for (i in parts) parts[i] = parts[i].split('=')`.

Lesson 19 Answers

1. To set an interrupt to occur at a specific time in the future, call the `setTimeout()` function, for example, `handle = setTimeout(DoThis, 5000)`. The object `handle` is saved for future control of the timeout.

2. To set interrupts to occur at repeating intervals, call the `setInterval()` function, for example, `handle = setInterval(DoThat, 1000)`.

3. To cancel a timeout from occurring, call the `clearTimeout()` function, passing the handle or (ID) of the timeout to cancel, for example, `clearTimeout(handle)`.

4. To cancel repeating interrupts from occurring, call the `clearInterval()` function, passing the handle (or ID) of the interval to cancel, for example, `clearInterval(handle)`.

5. The delay used for timeouts and intervals is milliseconds (thousandths of a second) so, for example, use a value of 1000 for 1 second.

6. To test whether a browser supports web workers, test the `worker` object of the current window, for example, `if (!!window.Worker) { /* Supported */ }`.

7. You can create a new web worker like this: `worker = new Worker('filename.js')`, where *filename.js* is the name of a file containing JavaScript to run in the background.

8. Web workers communicate with the calling process using the `onmessage` event of the worker object, for example, `worker.onmessage = function(event) { ... }`.

9. To send a message to the calling process, a web worker should call the `postMessage()` function, for example, `postMessage('This is a message')`.

10. The `data` property of the worker event object contains the posted message, for example, `worker.onmessage = function(event) { document .write(event.data) }`.

Lesson 20 Answers

1. To let JavaScript try out the three methods of creating an Ajax object in turn, the `try` keyword is used in conjunction with `catch()`.

2. Whenever an Ajax object's ready state changes, its `onreadystatechange` event is triggered.

3. The ready state of the `onreadystatechange` event is in its `readyState` property.

4. The status of the `onreadystatechange` event is in its `status` property.

5. The response text of the `onreadystatechange` event is in its `responseText` property.

6. The purpose of a callback function is to be called when a background process (such as an Ajax call) completes or has something to report.

7. You call a callback function using the `call()` function by attaching it to the callback function and passing any arguments necessary, for example, `callback.call(this.responseText)`.

8. It can be a good idea to add a random string to Ajax Get requests in order to prevent any caching proxy or other cache mechanism from serving up an older cached version of the requested page. Post requests are never cached and so this "trick" is not necessary for them.

9. To overwrite the HTML contents of an element, you write to its `innerHTML` property, for example, `mydiv.innerHTML = 'New DIV contents'`.

10. The supplied `OnDOMReady()` function is superior to using the built-in `onload()` function because it triggers earlier, meaning your JavaScript is called sooner, leading to a better user experience. However, be aware that although the DOM will be complete, not all document resources, such as images, may be loaded. If you need to access a particular image, for example, attach a function to the image's `onload` event.

Common JavaScript Functions

This appendix lists the most common functions and properties in JavaScript. The list is not fully comprehensive, however, as there are still a number of complex functions and properties that are beyond the scope of this book, due to requiring advanced programming techniques.

If you are interested in seeing what they are, though, you can download the addedbytes.com JavaScript cheat sheet at the following URL to act as a good starting point: tinyurl.com/jsfuncs.

Arithmetic Functions

- **Math.abs(a)**   Returns a as a positive number (or 0).
- **Math.acos(a)**   Returns the arc cosine of a.
- **Math.asin(a)**   Returns the arc sine of a.
- **Math.atan(a)**   Returns the arc tangent of a.
- **Math.atan2(a, b)**   Returns the arc tangent of a / b.
- **Math.ceil(a)**   Rounds up to return the integer closest to a.
- **Math.cos(a)**   Returns the cosine of a.
- **Math.exp(a)**   Returns the exponent of a (Math.E to the power a).
- **Math.floor(a)**   Rounds down to return the integer closest to à.
- **Math.log(a)**   Returns the log of a base e.
- **Math.max(a,b)**   Returns the maximum of a and b.
- **Math.min(a,b)**   Returns the minimum of a and b.
- **Math.pow(a,b)**   Returns a to the power b.
- **Math.random()**   Returns a pseudo-random number with a value of 0 or greater, but less than 1.
- **Math.round(a)**   Rounds up or down to return the integer closest to a.
- **Math.sin(a)**   Returns the sine of a.
- **Math.sqrt(a)**   Returns the square root of a.
- **Math.tan(a)**   Returns the tangent of a.

Array Functions

- **`array.concat(a2[, a3 …])`**   Returns a new array comprising `array` joined with a2 and optionally more arrays.
- **`array.every(c[, o])`**   Tests all elements of `array` using the callback function c, optionally using the object o as `this` when executing the callback.
- **`array.filter(c[, o])`**   Creates a new array with all elements in `array` that pass the test implemented by the function c, optionally using the object o as `this` when executing the callback.
- **`array.forEach(c[, o])`**   Calls callback function c for all elements in `array`, optionally using the object o as `this` when executing the callback.
- **`array.indexOf(s[, i])`**   Returns the first element of `array` that matches s, optionally starting at element index i (otherwise starting at element 0).
- **`array.join(s)`**   Returns a string comprising all elements in `array`, optionally joined to each other with the separator in string s (otherwise separated with a comma).
- **`array.lastIndexOf(s[, i])`**   Returns the last element of `array` that matches s, optionally working backward from element index i (otherwise starting at the end and working backward).
- **`array.map(c[, o])`**   Returns a new array comprising each element of `array` being passed to callback function c, optionally using the object o as `this` when executing the callback.
- **`array.pop()`**   Pops off the last element from `array` and returns it.
- **`array.push(e1[, e2 …])`**   Pushes element e1 (and optionally additional elements) to the end of `array`.
- **`array.reduce(c[, i])`**   Returns a single value determined by applying callback function c sequentially to each pair of elements in `array`, optionally using i as the initial argument to the first call of the callback. For example, if the callback function performs an addition and the array's contents are [1,2,3], then the result returned will be 6 (1 + 2 + 3).
- **`array.reduceRight(c[, i])`**   Same as reduce(), but `array` is processed in the opposite direction.
- **`array.reverse()`**   Returns `array` in reversed element order.
- **`array.shift()`**   Removes the first element from `array` and returns it.
- **`array.slice(s[, e])`**   Returns a new array comprising a selection of elements from `array` starting at index s and optionally ending at index e (otherwise ending at the array end).
- **`array.some(c[, o])`**   Tests whether at least one element of `array` passes the test in callback function c, optionally using the object o as `this` when executing the callback.
- **`array.toSource()`**   Returns a string representing the source code of `array`—not currently available in Internet Explorer or Safari.
- **`array.sort(f)`**   Returns `array` sorted using optional function f; otherwise, the array is sorted in case-sensitive, ascending alphabetical order.

- **array.splice(i, n[, e1 …])**   Returns an array extracted from `array` starting at index `i`, containing n elements from the array, and optionally adding the element `e1` (or more new elements).
- **array.toString()**   Returns a string representing the elements in `array` separated with commas.
- **array.unshift(e1[, e2 …])**   Adds `e1` (and optionally more elements) to the start of `array`, returning the new length of the array.

Boolean Functions

- **Boolean(n)**   Returns number n as a Boolean number.
- **object.toSource()**   Returns a string representing the source code of `object`—not currently available in Internet Explorer or Safari.
- **object.toString()**   Returns a string of either `true` or `false` depending on the value of `object`.
- **object.valueOf()**   Returns the primitive value of `object`.

Date Functions

- **Date()**   Returns a new `Date` object.
- **date.getDate()**   Returns the day of the month for `date` according to local time, between 1 and 31.
- **date.getDay()**   Returns the day of the week for `date` according to local time, between 0 for Sunday and 6 for Saturday.
- **date.getFullYear()**   Returns the year for `date` according to local time, as a four-digit number for years 1000–9999, such as 2018.
- **date.getHours()**   Returns the hour from `date` according to local time, between 0 and 23.
- **date.getMilliseconds()**   Returns the milliseconds from `date` according to local time, between 0 and 999.
- **date.getMinutes()**   Returns the minutes from `date` according to local time, between 0 and 59.
- **date.getMonth()**   Returns the month from `date` according to local time, between 0 for January and 11 for December.
- **date.getSeconds()**   Returns the seconds from `date` according to local time, between 0 and 59.
- **date.getTime()**   Returns the time in milliseconds since January 1, 1970, as 00:00:00 UTC.
- **date.getTimezoneOffset()**   Returns the difference, in minutes, between UTC and local time (can be negative, zero, or positive).
- **date.getUTCDate()**   Returns the day of the month from `date` according to Universal Time, between 1 and 31.

- **date.getUTCDay()**   Returns the day of the week from **date** according to Universal Time, between 0 for Sunday and 6 for Saturday.
- **date.getUTCFullYear()**   Returns the year from **date** according to Universal Time as a four-digit number for years 1000–9999, such as 2018.
- **date.getUTCHours()**   Returns the hour from **date** according to Universal Time, between 0 and 23.
- **date.getUTCMilliseconds()**   Returns the milliseconds from **date** according to Universal Time, between 0 and 999.
- **date.getUTCMonth()**   Returns the month from **date** according to Universal Time, between 0 for January and 11 for December.
- **date.getUTCSeconds()**   Returns the seconds from **date** according to Universal Time, between 0 and 59.
- **date.getYear()** *(Deprecated—use getFullYear() instead)*   Returns the year from **date** as a two-digit number.
- **date.setDate(d)**   Sets the day of the month in **date** according to local time, where d is between 1 and 31.
- **date.setFullYear(y[, m[, d]])**   Sets the year in **date** according to local time as a full year, such as 2018 in y, optionally passing the month between 0 and 11 in m, and the day between 1 and 31 in d.
- **date.setHours(h[, m[, s[, ms]]])**   Sets the hour in **date** according to local time, between 0 and 23 in h, optionally passing the minutes between 0 and 59 in m, the seconds between 0 and 59 in s, and the milliseconds between 0 and 999 in ms.
- **date.setMilliseconds(ms)**   Sets the milliseconds in **date** according to local time, where ms is between 0 and 999.
- **date.setMinutes(m[, s[, ms]])**   Sets the minutes in **date** according to local time, between 0 and 59 in m, optionally passing the seconds between 0 and 59 in s, and the milliseconds between 0 and 999 in ms.
- **date.setMonth(m[, d])**   Sets the month in **date** according to local time in m (from 0 for January to 11 for December), optionally passing the day (from 1 to 31) in d.
- **date.setSeconds(s[, ms])**   Sets the seconds in **date** according to local time, between 0 and 59 in s, optionally passing the seconds in milliseconds in ms.
- **date.setTime(t)**   Sets the time in **date** in milliseconds since January 1, 1970, at 00:00:00 UTC in t.
- **date.setUTCDate(d)**   Sets the day of the month in **date** according to Universal Time, between 1 and 31 in d.
- **date.setUTCFullYear(y[, m[, d]])**   Sets the year in **date** according to Universal Time, as a full year, such as 2018 in y, optionally passing the month between 0 and 11 in m, and the day between 1 and 31 in d.
- **date.setUTCHours(h[, m[, s[, ms]]])**   Sets the hour in **date** according to Universal Time, between 0 and 23 in h, optionally passing the minutes between 0 and 59 in m, the seconds between 0 and 59 in s, and the milliseconds between 0 and 999 in ms.

- `date.setUTCMilliseconds(ms)`   Sets the milliseconds in `date` according to Universal Time, between 0 and 999 in `ms`.
- `date.setUTCMinutes(m[, s[, ms]])`   Sets the minutes in `date` according to Universal Time, between 0 and 59 in `m`, optionally passing the seconds between 0 and 59 in `s`, and the milliseconds between 0 and 999 in `ms`.
- `date.setUTCMonth(m[, d])`   Sets the month in `date` according to Universal Time, between 0 for January and 11 for December in `m`, optionally passing the day between 1 and 31 in `d`.
- `date.setUTCSeconds(s[, ms])`   Sets the seconds in `date` according to Universal Time, between 0 and 59 in `s`, optionally passing the milliseconds between 0 and 999 in `ms`.
- `date.setYear(y)` *(Deprecated—use `setFullYear()` instead)*   Sets the year to a value from 1900 to 1999, where `y` is a value between 0 and 99.
- `date.toDateString()`   Returns the date from `date` according to local time, in human readable form in American English.
- `date.toGMTString()` *(Deprecated—use `toUTCString()` instead)*   Returns the date from `date` according to local time, using Internet GMT conventions.
- `date.toLocaleDateString()`   Returns the date from `date` according to local time, using the locale's conventions of the operating system.
- `date.toLocaleFormat(f)`   Returns the date from `date` according to local time, using the formatting specified in `f` (in the same format expected by the `strftime()` function in C)—not currently available in Internet Explorer or Safari.
- `date.toLocaleString()`   Returns the date from `date` according to local time, using the locale's conventions of the operating system.
- `date.toLocaleTimeString()`   Returns the time portion of the date from `date` according to local time, using the current locale's conventions.
- `date.toSource()`   Returns a string representing the source of `date`—not currently available in Internet Explorer or Safari.
- `date.toString()`   Returns the date (as a string) from `date`.
- `date.toTimeString()`   Returns the time portion of a date (as a string) from `date`.
- `date.toUTCString()`   Returns the date from `date` in the UTC time zone.
- `date.valueOf()`   Returns the primitive value of `date` as the number of milliseconds since midnight on January 1, 1970, UTC.

DOM Functions

- `document.createElement(t)`   Creates a new element with the tag name `t`.
- `document.getElementById(i)`   Returns the DOM object of the element with the id of `i`.
- `document.getElementsByTagName(t)`   Returns all elements matching the tag name in `t`.
- `document.write(s)`   Writes the value(s) in `s` to the browser; does not work in XHTML documents.

Global Functions

- **clearInterval(h)**   Clears the regular interrupts created by `setInterval()` using the handle in h.
- **clearTimeout(h)**   Clears the interrupt created by `setTimeout()` using the handle in h.
- **decodeURI(u)**   Returns the URI encoded string u as an unencoded string.
- **decodeURIComponent(u)**   Returns the URI component encoded string u as an unencoded string.
- **encodeURI(u)**   Returns the string u in URI encoded form without encoding URI reserved characters that have special meaning.
- **encodeURIComponent(u)**   Returns the string u in URI encoded form and encodes any characters that have special meaning in URIs, such as , , /, ?, :, @, &, =, +, $, and #.
- **escape(s)** (*Deprecated—use encodeURI() or encodeURIComponent() instead*)   Returns s encoded by escaping special characters.
- **eval(e)**   Returns the result of evaluating the expression in e.
- **function.call(a1[, a2 …])**   Calls the function `function` passing any number of optional arguments.
- **isFinite(v)**   Returns true if v is a finite, legal number, or false if it is infinite or NaN.
- **isNaN(v)**   Returns true if the value v is not a number; otherwise, returns false.
- **parseFloat(s)**   Returns the string s as a floating point number.
- **parseInt(s)**   Returns the string s as an integer.
- **setInterval(c, m)**   Sets up repeating interrupts calling the code in c every m milliseconds; returns a handle that can be used to clear the interrupts.
- **setTimeout(c, m)**   Sets up a single interrupt to call the code in c in m milliseconds; returns a handle that can be used to clear the interrupt.
- **unescape(s)** (*Deprecated - use decodeURI() or decodeURIComponent() instead*)   Returns the escaped string s as an unescaped string.

Number Functions

- **Number(s)**   Returns string s as a number.
- **number.constructor()**   Returns the function that created this instance of number; by default, this is the Number object.
- **number.toExponential(n)**   Returns a string representing number in exponential notation with n representing the number of digits after the decimal point.
- **number.toFixed(n)**   Formats number with n digits to the right of the decimal point.
- **number.toLocaleString()**   Returns a string value version of number in a format that may vary according to a browser's locale settings.

- `number.toPrecision(n)`   Returns a string representing number to the specified precision n.
- `number.toString(n)`   Returns a string representation of number in the specified radix (base) in n.
- `number.valueOf()`   Returns the primitive value of number.

Regular Expression Functions

- `regex.exec(s)`   Returns an array of matches found in the string s using the regular expression regex, or returns null if no matches were made.
- `regex.test(s)`   Tests the string s using the regular expression regex, returning true if a match is found, otherwise false.
- `regex.toSource()`   Returns a string representing the source code of regex—not currently available in Internet Explorer or Safari.
- `regex.toString()`   Returns a string representation of regex in the form of a regular-expression literal.

String Functions

- `String(n)`   Returns number n as a string.
- `string.charAt(n)`   Returns the character in string at index n.
- `string.charCodeAt(n)`   Returns a number indicating the Unicode value of string at index n.
- `string.concat(s1[, s2 …])`   Concatenates string with s1 (and more strings if passed) and returns a new single string.
- `string.indexOf(s[, i])`   Returns the index in string of the search string s, optionally starting at i.
- `string.lastIndexOf(s[, i])`   Returns the index in string of the last occurrence of search string s, optionally starting at i.
- `string.localeCompare(s)`   Returns a number indicating whether string comes before or after (or is the same) as s in sort order.
- `string.match(e)`   Returns one or more matches (depending on whether the g modifier is used in the expression) for the regular expression e in the string string.
- `string.replace(e, s)`   Finds a match between regular expression e and string string.
- `string.search(e)`   Returns the index of the first location of regular expression e in string string.
- `string.slice(s[, e])`   Extracts a section of string starting at index s, and optionally ending at e (otherwise ending at the string end).
- `string.split(s[, l])`   Returns an array comprising sections of string split at separator s, optionally limited to the number of occurrences specified in l.

- `string.substr(s[, l])`   Returns a section of `string` starting from index `s`, and optionally limited to the number of characters in `l`; otherwise, all characters to the end of the string are returned.
- `string.substring(f, t)`   Returns a substring of `string` starting from index `f` and ending with the character immediately preceding index `t`.
- `string.toLocaleLowerCase()`   Returns a lowercase version of `string` according to the current locale.
- `string.toLocaleUpperCase()`   Returns an uppercase version of `string` according to the current locale.
- `string.toLowerCase()`   Returns a lowercase version of `string`.
- `string.toString()`   Returns a string representing `string`.
- `string.toUpperCase()`   Returns an uppercase version of `string`.
- `string.valueOf()`   Returns the primitive value of `string`.

Window Functions

- `alert(v)`   Pops up an alert window displaying the value(s) in `v`.
- `confirm(t)`   Pops up an alert window displaying the value in `t` and supplying two options: "OK" that returns `true` if clicked, and "Cancel" that returns `false` if clicked.
- `window.blur()`   Removes focus from window.
- `window.close()`   Closes `window`.
- `window.focus()`   Gives focus to window.
- `window.open(u, n[, f[, r]])`   Opens a new window using the URL in `u` and giving it the name in `n`. Optionally, the string `f` defines features such as height and width using a range of key/value pairs, and (optionally) either `true` or `false` in `r` if the window is to replace the current value in the browser's history (ignored by some browsers).
- `window.print()`   Opens a dialog for printing `window` to a printer.
- `window.scroll(x, y)`   The same as `scrollTo()` (see later).
- `window.scrollBy(x, y)`   Scrolls the window by `x` pixels horizontally and `y` pixels vertically.
- `element.scrollIntoView(a)`   Scrolls the element `element` into view, aligned to the window top if the optional argument `a` is `true`, otherwise aligned to the bottom.
- `window.scrollTo(x, y)`   Scrolls the window to the offset from the top left of the page of `x` pixels horizontally and `y` pixels vertically.

Index

A